SPII

DEVELOPMENT IN 5D

THE ROAD TO ENCHANTMENT SERIES

Gillian England

MYSTIC HEALING THERAPIES

BOOK TWO

TABLE OF CONTENTS

INTRODUCTION

One way or another, we've all be duped. Duped by the governments, the health care system, the education system, the tax systems, the mainstream media, the list goes on and on. But lets face it, vaxxed or un-vaxxed each and every one of us has been lied to, conned, tricked, coerced. They have poisoned our food, our water, torn apart our communities, and have even used the elements against us, with the harp weather manipulation machines, not to mention deliberately spraying our skies with poisonous chemtrails, that block out the sunshine and deposit harmful chemicals on us.

It really is a miracle that we have survived this onslaught, and that's before I mention that we have all been wage slaves, one way or another in modern day slavery, working for "the system", being unlawfully taxed here there and everywhere.

This has been going on for not just hundreds but thousands of years, and if you've just woken up to what's been going on, it can look pretty gloomy and hopeless. But the good news is, their time is up! It has been written in the scriptures of old, and astrologically, the age of Aquarius is upon us. It's time for the old controllers, to leave the planet. Thirteen families have basically been controlling and enslaving humanity, but now they are on their last legs. The light on our beautiful planet earth is getting brighter and lighter with each passing day. And as it does, more and more people are waking up from their slumber and seeing the truth, and as their consciousness evolves, it inevitably starts to raise esoteric questions, which leads on to consideration of ones spiritual life.

Spirituality and consciousness are very different from religion. All organised religion has been designed to control and diminish humanity, to make them believe they are un-pure, unworthy, and need a middle man to access God. Organised religions are little more than money-making, controlling institutes, that fill us with guilt and a sense of lack or sin. The purity of the original teachings, like everything else has been hijacked. I'm not saying that there aren't good people who follow the religions, but I am saying that all religion is fraudulent, and designed to mis-lead the masses. Spirituality on the other hand, requires no middle man, we are all capable of connecting our own unique connection to God/source, there are universal principles that guide this, but spirituality is free from dogma, and harsh rules.

As well as all the things I mentioned above, we have all been lied to, with regard to our true natures as human beings. Each and every one of us, is a magical powerful being, capable of so much more that we have been told. The thing is, in order for the former controllers of the world to be able to control us, they needed to keep us thinking that we were insignificant and powerless, nothing could be further from the truth. Many of us now know that anything the government and mainstream media tells us is safe and good for us, clearly isn't (covid jab) and anything they tell us is bad for us is good (sunshine). Well it's been the same with respect of the true nature of our spirituality. I'm guessing that many of you here, up until two or three years ago, probably felt spiritual stuff, such as spiritual mediums, tarot, crystals, energy healing, natural healing remedies, ley lines, and even extra terrestrials was a bit weird, a bit "woo woo", for new age hippies, or mad cat ladies. Perhaps the idea of a spiritual life felt a bit uncomfortable, or not even relevant in a busy world. Like everything else, the former controllers, did a great job of marketing the above, as things weird people do, and gave them a flavour of mistrust, they purposely did this, to stop people investigating these routes, to keep them disconnected from their soul-selves.

Currently we are in the midst of a mass great awakening, partly due to the light keys and codes being emitted from the sun. There are new sun's available to us now from the solar system, which are assisting in the great awakening of ordinary people, people whom ten years ago would not have given spirituality any attention at all. There are masses of organic humans now ready to step into their true power, their true identity, and finding their sense of spirituality is key to this.

I've had the good fortune to have been awake from birth, and the even better fortune to have been sent to a Spiritualist Sunday school as a child. Back then in the 1970's at the Spiritualist Lyceums we were taught things like dimensions, astral plains, manifesting, as well as spiritual phenomena such as clairvoyance and clairaudience.

I am also dyslexic, hopeless at spelling, and I often pronounce words incorrectly, now I realise that this was to prevent me from becoming spell-cast, and programmed, as now I understand that MK ultra, and linguistic programming used by the military and the media, are specifically designed to programme and control the behaviour of the masses. (Think the UK government covid hoax advertising "look into my eyes....") I have always naturally had a strong connection to spirit, and I have my difficult childhood to sincerely thank for this. We all chose our life-paths and soul contract prior to birth, and I now realise that I chose very well, because I reached adulthood, with not a single care about what other people thought of me, as long as I can stand before God and myself, then that's all that matters to me. This is very liberating! When the covid hoax hit, I was very comfortable not wearing a mask even though I got chased down in shopping malls and supermarkets by gestapo security staff. I wonder how many people gave their lives to the vax just because of concern about what other people think of them?

Our thoughts, behaviours and words create our lives, and our underlying philosophies on life, govern our decisions about how we conduct ourselves. With this in mind, it is useful to consider where you have got your rules and standards from? For example, if we take our philosophy from social media and day time television, (tell lie vision) then what sort of standards and principles are we going to adopt? I would wager, not very healthy ones, the past few years has shown us that when they tell us something is safe and good for us, invariably it's the opposite. If on the other hand we hold our own personal philosophy, derived from a strong connection to God/source, then we will be much better equipped to lead happy, healthy, abundant lives, more akin to 5D living.

WHAT IS 3D, 4D, 5D?

This refers to the dimensional space in which forms our current reality. For the most part, for the past thousands of years, we have been living under the illusion of 3D living. This is where we believe that all that there is, would be visible to our eyes, a world where we think we need "evidence" to prove something exists. In 3D, time is linear, ie, You are born you have a life, you die, the time goes from point A to point B in a straight line. In 3D, esoteric things are viewed as fanciful, merely of the imagination, or something that you need a priest, or guru to access. Matter rules, and to change the structure of matter, requires hands on work to create and build it. 3D life is hard work, often toiling long hour each day, just to earn enough resource to provide a roof over your head and enough food to live on, we were never meant to be wage slaves!. If your vibrational rate is consistent to 3D, chances are you will be largely self-interested, believe the governments have our best interests at heart, love the royal family, be fully engaged with social media dramas, love watching the news channels, TV and listening to celebrity gossip, these will subconsciously guide your rules for living and philosophies.

If on the other hand your vibrational rate is more akin to 5D, you will naturally want to help others, you will love nature and will be more naturally attuned to spiritual matters. You will be able to see through the media and government lies and propaganda, and may have stepped into your power as a sovereign man or woman of this land. Many of you reading this will already be vibrating on a 5D level, but we acknowledge that we are still living in a 3D world, we have to flip flop between the two currently, as many of us have jobs and commitments that are firmly in the 3D paradigm, however, we can still approach the 3D aspects of our lives keeping our 5D vibration in tact.

There is much talk currently about the ascension, and moving to 5D, if you are new to all this, it can seem a bit confusing as to what all this means. Basically, what this means is, when there are enough people vibrating at a 5D level of vibration, the scalar effect will catapult us into a 5D world instead of where we are currently in the 3D. What I mean by the scalar effect, is like a tipping point, when enough of us reach that level, the scales will tip to 5D. That's why it is important that we all take personal responsibility to live our best 5D lives. Many people have been programmed to believe statements such as "what difference can my efforts make alone", but this could not be further from the truth. It takes many tiny droplets to make an ocean, once there are enough individual droplets of 5D energy in that ocean, then the entire ocean becomes 5D. In 5D life is much fairer, we are not wage slaves toiling to scratch out a meagre existence, we live in abundance, with free natural resources, free food, free energy, free travel. We have the time to engage in arts, socialise, dance, sing, do things that make us happy. Mother earth has created abundance for all her children, it is only the dark forces that have hijacked this, and plundered our natural resources, but the dark forces cannot survive in 5D, they will be left behind in 3D, to work out their karma. In 5D, spiritually forms the basis of our entire lives. We create by thinking positively, we all have the potential to be creator beings, it's just a case of accessing this innate knowledge that is imprinted in our DNA. As our vibration increases, more strands of DNA will be available to us, therefore, we will be able to access more of our spiritual gifts and talents.

SO WHAT ABOUT 4D?

4D is the in between stage, like the bridge between the two dimensions. To put simply, many people who I would consider 4D, may be awake to the government propaganda, but be totally ignorant of the spiritual context of it all. Devoid of any spiritual knowledge and power, for these people life looks all doom and gloom, they are constantly stuck in a cycle of anxiety and fear about the Armageddon future that they perceive to be their reality.

Equally many of the love and light brigade are also stuck in 4D, they may have pseudo spiritual lives, where they deny anything that they consider negative. They believe all that the governments tell them is for their best interests, have been avid mask wearers, and have rolled up their sleeves in the past few years multiple times, eat bugs, and may choose electric cars. They would not want to acknowledge any darkness, so would deny that satanic rituals and child trafficking is a real thing. Remember, this is programming from the dark forces, get people to deny it's existence, then it protects the perpetrators. This is 4D vibration, despite sitting on yoga mats wafting incense and wearing "spiritual clothing".

Another aspect of the 4D realm is the lower astral plains, what I mean by this is when we die, i.e leave our physical bodies, if we get stuck between the realms, we may end up in 4D as ghosts. Lower entities such as ghouls and goblins also live in this dimension, it is not a place on which you would want to hang around. Over the years, I have done much work, freeing and releasing entities and discarnate humans that were stuck in 4D, I have helped them traverse this realm, and reach the light. Often people who pass to spirit during traumatic circumstances get stuck in 4D. Whilst travelling through France, I have freed up and released the souls of platoons of world war I soldiers, that had got trapped in the horrors of war, in the 4th dimension. I remember once freeing the soul of a little girl that had fallen into a well many, many years before, and had not realised she had "died", I also remember freeing up a soul that had been "walled in", deliberately and cruelly been sealed into a wall, whilst still alive!.. These are examples of who and what may be existing on the 4th dimension.

CHAPTER 1

PRACTICAL EXERCISES TO DEVELOP YOUR SPIRITUALITY

GETTING STARTED

All organic human beings have a magical enchanted blue-print, that is encoded into our DNA. We all have it, it's just that some people are more open to receiving the magic than others. The aim of this book, is to enable you to open up, and step into your own divine space, to enable you to tap into your own enchanted earth. It is very easy to understand and takes a practical down to earth approach, the exercises and spiritual practices in this book are accessible for everyone. With a clear intention, spiritual discipline and an open heart, the sky isn't even the limit to where you may find yourself!

So how do we find ourselves in this magical, space? It starts by opening up to the spirit world, expanding our consciousness, increasing our susceptibility and connectivity to the field of consciousness of everything that has ever been, is and ever was. You will hear me talking a lot about frequency and vibration. Each and every one of us is emitting a unique light code from our etheric body, some of you may think of this as your aura, I use the terms auric field, energetic field, etheric body, it all means the same thing.

The more spiritually evolved we become, the higher the light and the larger our auric field/energetic field radiates, you could say that your vibration gets higher. That's why you might of heard of the term "high vibed". Along with this, as we evolve, we naturally activate more strands of our DNA. "Scientists" refer to junk DNA, it isn't junk at all, it's just not activated. The way we activate it, is by being able to hold more light in our energetic field. The way we get more light in our energetic field is to evolve our spiritual natures. Remember, our spiritual selves are the divine parts of our nature, it's only in the later cycles of earth, that many have disconnected to the spiritual side of ourselves, and anything spiritual has been seen as an "extra" at best or "weird" at worse. The aim of this book is to help you enhance your spiritual natures, and step into your divine magical, spiritual selves.

Every spiritual practice needs to start with a clear intention. Some people might call this "opening the sacred space" "opening prayers" or "invocation". It doesn't matter what you call it, the main thing is the intention you set, as this will set the entire vibration for the proceedings.

We need to be sure that we are opening a space that is of the highest light, and that we are only calling in beings that have the highest and best intentions for all concerned at heart. For example, if you were going out for the day would you leave the front door of your home open for anyone and everyone to wander in? Doubtful, most likely you would lock your door, and when you were at home you would only invite people in that were friendly and benign and that were sure not to wreck havoc. It's the same for any sort of spiritual practice, be crystal clear of your intention, invite only those of the highest and best intentions for all concerned.

Many of us have been taught by religion, that we need to access God or the spiritual realms via some human that has assumed a position of power, i.e priest, vicar, pope, inman, minister, guru or via Jesus, Mohammad, Mahatma etc. The truth of the matter is, we don't need the middle man, we can all go directly to source. This is a secret they didn't want you to know, because knowing this puts you in touch your own divine power, instead of relying on some external source. In our new earth, a big lesson for us all is personal responsibility, we are all master of our own ship, we take responsibility for every aspect of our lives, including our connectivity to God.

OPENING UP A SCARED SPACE

There are a few pointers of good practice, but other than that, there are no hard and fast rules about what opening a sacred space would sound like. If the invocation is personal to you, and from the heart, that's all that matters.

The points you would be wise to consider are:

- Call in Archangel Michael and ask for protection, then call in anyone else you wish to help, it could be your guides, angels, dragons, whoever you work with. If you are new to this, just call in Archangel Michael to start with, as time progresses you will become aware of who your team are.

- Make it clear that you are calling in those with only the highest and best intentions for all concerned

- State your intention for the practice, i.e to help heal your pet dog, or to rejuvenate the land, or help you accept wisdom for your spiritual journey, what ever your reason for connecting, state it clearly.

- Thank your helpers for joining you today. (At the end of the practice we always offer thanks, this will be covered later in the book).

Here are some examples of how I might open up to spirit, Part 1 is the general opening, part 2 (multiple examples) states the specific intention for the day, remember, this is only my way of doing it, it is not the golden standard, you will have your own way!

Part 1 - *Great Spirit, Divine Light of Source, I connect with you today with love and harmony in my heart, and give thanks and gratitude for all my earthly experiences. I ask for Archangel Michael to shield me with his cloak of protection, and know his sword also offers me protection. I call in my dragons, Archangel Raphael, unicorns, higher galactics, elementals and spirits of this place. I give thanks to all for their love and service.*

Part 2 - Example A - *Great Spirit, today I link with you, and ask that I may be open to the divine guidance, that I fulfil my soul mission, and am able to bring forth the vibration of your love and wisdom to all whom I come into contact with today. With much gratitude, thank you.*

Part 2 – Example B - *Great Spirit, I link with you today, with the intention of clearing this space, please enable me to return this land, to it's original divine frequency. Using my free will, of my organic human presence, incarnated on this earth, please help me to clear this space of any energy that does not serve the highest and best intention for all concerned. With much gratitude, thank you.*

Part 2 – Example C - *Great Spirit, I link with you today, simply to say thank you for everything. I give special thanks to the elementals in my garden that have given it such colour and splendour, thank you elementals. I also give special thanks to my dragons and the angelic team, thanks for your energy and thanks for your love and protection. I also give thanks to everyone in my life that has offered me a chance to grow and learn. This has not always been an easy path, but I recognise now, that many of those challenges have helped me grow and develop, so I give thanks for them too.*

NOW YOU HAVE OPENED UP A SPACE WHAT NEXT?

Now we've opened up a space, we can start to expand our conscious awareness, by calming down our nervous system, disengaging from the noise of our dominate analytical over-thinking left brain, and begin to create a space that is amiable to connecting to both spirit, and our own soul memory, over-soul, higher self. To start with, a simple breathing meditation is an excellent place to begin.

There are no gimmicks or fast tracks to developing your consciousness as this depends on the amounts of light your crystalline body is able to hold, which in turn activates more strands of your DNA. The more of your DNA you have activated, the more "spiritual gifts" will be available to you. It is true that undertaking an iowaska ceremony can enable you to see through the fog of the 3D lies, and can assist awakening. However, it is not able to help you activate your DNA per se. Sometimes people go through an awakening of the soul as a result of what they saw during their iowaska experience, but the iowaska didn't do the work for them, they will still have to go through the process of connecting their own consciousness to spirit, bringing in and holding the light in their own bodies, and activating their own DNA. We are learning a big lesson in personal responsibility, it's exactly the same with spiritual development, we can't rely on an external source to do it for us, it comes from within.

BREATHING MEDITATION

For maximum benefit, I would recommend doing this exercise for ten minutes per day to start with, ideally 5 days out of 7. As well as the physiological benefits of calming down your nervous system, lowering your blood pressure, and soothing your mind, this also shows your spirit team that you are committed to working with them.

Begin by sitting quietly and taking in some nice deep breaths, breathing in through your nose, and out through your mouth. Imagine all the cares of the day leaving you. Place your focus of attention on the little space behind the top of your nose (inside your nose, when you take a breath in through your nose, this is the place you feel the air entering your airways). Simply keep your focus of attention on that place in your nose. Don't try to alter your natural breathing pattern in any way, just breath. If your mind wonders off, just acknowledge the wondering thought, let it go, then bring your focus of attention back to your nose. Be gentle with yourself, if you are new to meditation it can seem daunting. Be persistent even if you are bombarded by your thoughts, be loving to yourself, acknowledge the thought, let it go, and refocus on that point at the back of your nose. Avoid attaching any shoulds/shouldn'ts to your thoughts i.e "I shouldn't keep thinking about work" or "I should be able to do this better", that's old programming, let it go, gently steer your attention back to that spot behind the top of your nose.

Once you find yourself in the rhythm of this, you might want to take it a bit further, for example you could mindfully think about letting go of your stress on the out breath, and breathing in love or tranquillity on the in breath. Another way of doing this is to use colour, depending on what meaning you have attached for each colour, you could imagine breathing in a certain colour that you feel would be beneficial, and breathing out any colour that isn't serving you. I have used this method to breath out minor illnesses, lets say I had a cold, I would imagine the energy of the cold as deep dark black smoke, I would image breathing this out on the out breath, then I would imagine breathing in a sunshine ray, and would imagine the sunshine ray rejuvenating my body. It can also be a very useful tool to help breath out anger or emotional pain. Imagine your anger or emotional pain as black smoke, see it leaving your body on the out-breath, then see a beautiful fresh colour entering in on the in breath. This can be a very powerful, self-healing method, give it a go!

I would recommend giving the breathing meditation a try, after all, spiritual development requires discipline and commitment, so by persisting with this, shows you are serious about your development. A big part of opening up your psychic and spiritual abilities relies on trusting your intuition and when you see something in your minds eye, or when you get an impression or a feeling, you don't dismiss it as just your imagination. In order to do this, you need to have cleared the decks so to speak, so this is why quieting the mind, and reducing the dominance of the left brain is so important. You won't develop spiritually by thinking and intellectualising, it comes from open heartedness, and open minds, the breathing meditation is a gateway to this.

Grounding – As we begin to open ourselves up to the spiritual realms it is imperative to learn the art of grounding. The more we connect to spirit, the more time we will spend with our consciousness expanded out into our multi-dimensional space. It's all very well doing this, but we need to be able to come back into our bodies, and carry on living in the 3D realm too. If we are not grounded, then we are not anchoring in the light to the planet, and that is the whole point of being a light warrior – to bring in light through your light body, and anchor it into the earth. When new to spiritual awakening, it is tempting to constantly daydream, and have your consciousness floating about in spiritual space, but again, the point of us being in the human body is to marry the two together, both the spiritual and the physical. To do this, we need to have mastered grounding, and we will most definitely need to have done this, by the time we step into our fully functioning 5D multi-dimensional selves.

If you are not fully grounded, you may find yourself being clumsy or accident prone. First thing in a morning I am both of these until I have had my breakfast. I've never had any problems with blood sugar levels or anything like that, it is simply due to the fact that during sleep state I go off planet battling demons etc. so when I get back I need something to eat and drink to bring me back to earth, it's the same after I've sat for channelling sessions.

There are few techniques I would recommend; After you have engaged in a meditation, or a spiritual practice, imagine from the souls of your feet (your earth star chakra), that you grow roots down into the ground, like tree roots, spreading out, and anchoring you steadfastly into the earth, this is good way of ending your spiritual practice. From a physical behavioural point of view, try taking a walk bare foot onto the earth, be it grass, the beach, anywhere, where the bare souls of your feet can touch the earth. Go for a wild swim, or at least paddle in the ocean, river, stream, this will connect you to the earth, especially if you consciously engage with the water whilst doing so. If you have a garden, or even some plant pots, put your hands in the soil, touch the earth, connect with it.

Another technique is to look at your present environment, and look for five things from where abouts you are, that you haven't noticed before. Come into the here and now moment by observing details about your current place. For example, if I was stood in my office, I might notice how the trees over the road make a shape like a face, I may notice the sound of the wind howling, I may take notice of the smell of the coffee from the kitchen, or feel the softness of the chair I am sitting on. Engage the 5 senses of the here and now, it will bring you back to earth.

And finally, believe it or not swearing is excellent for grounding. A few choice words will bring you smack back to earth ****!

FURTHER TIPS TO HELP QUIETEN THE MIND AND RAISE YOUR VIBRATION

Nature - In addition to the breathing meditation, there are numerous other things you can do, that will serve the purpose of quieting that left brain dominant thinking. One of the best things ever is to get out in nature. I absolutely adore nature, you will find me outside in all weathers, enjoying the serene beauty of my surroundings, talking to the trees, the birds, the insects. The wonderous outdoors is already vibrating at a 5D frequency, so by bathing in the energy of the natural world, your frequency will naturally start to match the vibrational level of your surroundings. There are a few things to do that will assist this.

Firstly, where possible, leave your electronic devices at home. If this is not possible, then at least switch off the device, to minimise EMF. Focus on the here and now, as mentioned in the grounding exercise above, for example, you might notice that the river curves in a particular way, or that the window box has pretty patterns in the wood grain. Really get in touch with the details. This will bring you to the present moment, which is another helpful tool, in terms of spiritual progression. In the 3D world, we spend much of our time either fast forwarding our thoughts onto possible future scenarios, this can cause anxiety, or we ruminate over the past, that can cause depression or a feeling of lack, both of these lower your vibration. On the other hand by living in the present moment, we are truly engaging with our experience, and helping to keep our frequency in tact.

Another thing you can do is really listen to nature, can you hear birds? What do you imagine they are saying to you? Several years ago I had an experience where I must have been naturally aligned with the oneness field of consciousness, when I heard a Jackdaw (type of crow) literally shout "Evacuate! I was startled, and It took me a moment or two to realise it was actually a bird, and not a person yelling at me! If I'm out and about and a particular bird catches my attention, I will telepathically communicate to it, and ask it what it's message is. If a bird or animal catches your attention, start by imagining what it is saying to you, trust in your impressions, and as your consciousness develops you will be able to decode the messages with more grace and ease. Birdsong is very high vibrational, so if you are fortunate enough to live in an area with song birds, open your windows, and allow the beautiful song to journey you to a higher state.

Insects and bees are also messengers, and keepers of frequency. Bees emit a divine frequency code, so by actively listening to them buzzing can help raise your own vibration. Take time to tune into their sound, let it flow through your being, it will help your alignment. I am constantly thanking nature for being here, If I hear pollinators, I will thank them for their divine service.

I love trees, such wise old souls, they are like giant battery packs, huge holders of high frequencies and knowledge, that withstands time. Trees do a great service to humanity and the entire planet, by literally holding high frequencies and knowledge, and embedding them into the fabric of the earth. Their root systems, connect over vast distances, holding and keeping steady the energies. I am certain that often, trees root themselves in ley lines. On multiple occasions when I've seen a particular striking wise old tree, I have checked this with my divining rods, and more times than not, they are on ley lines or energy points. Sitting under a tree, or choosing a favourite tree and building up a relationship with it is a wonderful way of connecting with the spiritual realms, and calming down your mind. Many indigenous cultures, such as Native Americans and Celts of Britain, would have communicated with trees on a daily basis, this would be seen as normal and natural, it's only in these latter times that doing this would be seen as odd.

The natural world is a wonderful messenger, and is already tuned into unity consciousness, finding time to connect with nature, will help your spiritual development enormously. Even if you live in a big city, there will still be areas of nature available, the sky, the parks, the river, even window boxes and house plants can put you in touch with nature's vibration.

Dancing/Shamanic Drumming/Singing - Practically all indigenous cultures engage in ritual singing, dancing and drumming. All of these activities raise the vibrational level of both the space and the participants. During the fake covid era, all these activities were banned in most parts of the world, that's because they knew the positive impact of these activities on frequencies, and when you are trying to control a population by keeping their vibration low, the last thing they want you doing is enjoying yourself dancing, singing and drumming!

Any sort of movement in your body can help shift stuck energy, going for a walk, yoga, tai chi, are all good for your vibration, as well as your mood, fitness and well-being. Dancing can be a great tonic for low mood, and lethargy. We have been socially conditioned to be self-conscious of our dance moves, many people won't dare dance in public (unless having consumed alcohol) for fear of being judged, or criticised. This is 3D conditioning, in our new 5D world, everyone will have the confidence to move freely. Being concerned about other's opinions of you is the ego playing out, once you've gotten rid of the unhelpful aspects of the ego, you won't care less about what others think of you.

I used to be part of a wonderful shamanic drumming group, that met monthly at a local village hall. We would honour the Celtic seasons and festivals, honour mother earth, and grandfather sky, it was a wonderful community. Unfortunately when the fake covid hit, the organisers fell for the media propaganda, and were asking for proof of vaccination to attend. Therefore I had to walk away from that. Another loss, but on the positive side, losing our former communities and friends drove us to find others on the same vibrational level, everyone reading or listening to this work is part of that new community. Thank you for being here!

Music and singing can be a great way to access higher levels of vibration and consciousness. I've had the privilege to visit the great halls of music in the etheric realms, words cannot do justice to the sublime frequencies emanated there. On a percentage scale, even the most beautiful soul-touching music experienced on the earth currently, would not even be 2% of what's available on the higher realms.

However, just like everything else, believe it or not, music too, has been used as a weapon against us by the dark cult. They have done this by deliberately recording all the music you hear today, from your radios, downloads, CD's, etc. to the frequency of 440 hertz which is in direct opposition to our natural state. Therefore, even by listening to a pleasant melody, that you think might be uplifting you, can in fact cause some irritation and discourse to your vibration. Some enlightened artists, such as Garath Icke (David Icke's son) are aware of this, and have purposely recorded their music on the frequency of 432 hertz which is aligned to our vibration, and therefore does not assault your frequency whilst listening to it.

On another note, talking of sounds and vibration, here in the UK the emergency services sirens (ie ambulance, police, fire) are all set at a frequency that will engender the most primal fear in a human. Using these sirens liberally, ensures a constant attack on our vibration. When I hear these sirens, I consciously say to myself I do not consent to having my vibration lowered, and visualise the sound bouncing off my auric field, in this way I am stepping into my own power, and are not allowing anyone or anything lower my frequency. If we want to make positive changes, the first steps are always to have an awareness of the problem. I refuse to feel the victim in any situation, that is very disempowering, instead I recognise the problem (i.e sirens designed to keep our frequency lower) then I state clearly that I do not consent, followed by visualising my energy field remaining in tact. This is how we empower ourselves folks, why not give it a try?

CHAPTER 2

DEVELOPING YOUR PSYCHIC AWARENESS

As we start to expand our consciousness, we will naturally have more access to our psychic abilities. Having developed psychic abilities means that you are able to tap into the unified field of consciousness and decode the universal information that is available for everyone. The way you tap into the unified field of consciousness may come in several different forms, you may of heard of terms such as;

- **Clairvoyant** the literal translation of this means clear vision. This is where you get psychic impressions of things seen as a vision. For example, if I asked you to imagine a pink elephant, in your minds eye you are seeing a pink elephant. That's what a clairvoyant image looks like. You are not seeing an actual pink elephant stood directly in front of you, you are seeing it in your minds eye.

- **Clairaudient** this means clear hearing. This is where you hear voices, or you might actually hear your guides talking to you. You could actually hear their voices as though they are sat in the room with you. But again you may hear them in your imagination. For example, right now imagine your best friend is talking to you wishing you a happy birthday, you can hear them in your imagination, even though your best friend isn't sat in front of you right now. (I would re-iterate the importance of opening up a sacred space before engaging in any spiritual practice, this way any voices you hear will have the highest and best intention for all concerned).

- **Clairsentient** this means clear sensing/clear feeling. If you are clairsentient you may be able to feel and sense what's going on in the field. For example, you may be able to feel that your friend is going through a bad patch, even though you've not seen or spoken to her for several weeks. You can feel it in your own psychic field. You may be very sensitive to energies. For example, if you walked into a room where someone had just had a big argument, even though it was quiet at the time, you would be able to feel the residual energy of the argument.

- **Claircognizant** means clear knowing. The 3D paradigm has conditioned everyone to want " scientific evidence" for everything. When you are claircognizant, you just know things, you know truths and often are not quite sure how you know it! But you won't have any "evidence" for your truths, because this is coming from a higher level, often your higher self. In the 3D we have been conditioned to dismiss this knowing as just your imagination. But I would like to assure you, that if this knowing is coming from deep within the core of your being, then chances are it's your truth, have confidence in your abilities to discern the truth, even if it doesn't make any sense to the 3D "scientists".

You may already be aware of your spiritual gifts, and already be very familiar with the above. Or you may just be at the start of your spiritual journey. Either way it doesn't matter, it is not a race or a competition. If anyone is feeling superior to another, based on their perceived spiritual stance, or based on how long they believe they've been "awake", then they are clearly not as advanced as they believe themselves to be.

In 5D there is no place for the duality of superior/inferior. If one is feeling superior on some level, then they are clearly in the duality of better/lesser, which means on some level they will be feeling lesser than others, a very disempowering stance to be in. Also the duality of superior/inferior leaves one vulnerable to the idea of gurus. Again this is a 3D concept, if you put someone on a spiritual pedestal, and blindly follow their teachings, without first checking in with your own discernment, you are disregarding your own sense of right/wrong, and giving away your personal power.

In our 5D world, it is all about us as individuals stepping into our own sense of self, and sense of power, not blindly following others. There is nothing wrong with appreciating someone's work or teachings, like appreciating someone's art work, or cooking, but would you blindly follow a celebrity chef, and stop eating foods that are to your own tastes just because the celebrity chef suggested you did? Chances are you would try the dish, if it was to your taste and made you feel good, you would repeat the recipe, on the other hand if it wasn't to your taste you would not adopt the recipe. I recommend you consider adopting the same philosophy when it comes to spiritual teachers, myself included!

As your vibration raises, naturally you will find accessing your spiritual gifts gets easier. However, I do want to add here, that just because you can communicate with spirit, doesn't automatically mean you are high vibrational. I've known spiritual mediums who are firmly stuck in the 3D realm of duality, engaging with the superior/inferior hegemony, even though they had the ability to bring forth uncle Alfred and aunty Dorothy from the spirit world.

PRACTICAL EXERCISES

So far we have covered opening up a safe spiritual space, and looked at raising vibrational levels via meditation, dance, music, drumming, nature etc. Now lets look at some little games you can play with yourself and friends, in order to sharpen up, and hone in on your psychic awareness. There are loads of little opportunities you can take throughout the day, that can test your psychic ability without anyone knowing you are doing it. For example, next time you hear your phone ringing, guess who it is before you pick it up. If you are out driving your car, guess what colour the next car you see will be. If you follow soccer or a particular sport, guess what the result will be. If you are at work, guess which colleague will walk through the door next. If you are out in nature, guess what the next bird you see/hear will be.

Be creative, decide your own guesses, that fit with your lifestyle and situation. Although it may seem like a little private guessing game, in fact what you are doing is expanding your consciousness into the field of everything that ever was/is. You are in effect projecting your psychic senses out into the field, and attempting to decode the field, by seeing what you pick up. The 3D world would say that your answers were based on probability, but remember we aren't playing by 3D rules anymore. The more you practice this, the more accurate you will find your answers to be. The beauty of this game, is that you can continually practice this, without anyone knowing, and you are not worried if you are right or wrong, because only you will know.

A little story I have around this, my in-laws loved to play card games and board games, their favourites were maths games. I am absolutely rubbish at maths, even though I have two post-graduate degrees, I could not even pass the general school certificate in maths, despite my huge efforts. Therefore I could never win the maths games they played. However, sometimes we would play games that relied on blindly picking counters, or certain cards. I used my psychic abilities, to tune in, and pick up the cards that were favourable to me, and I always won those games. The more you practice, the better you get.

I just need to mention here that the universe has it's own wisdom in such matters, because we were only playing for fun, I was able to use my psychic abilities to win these games. However, if I would have tried this trick at a casino to try to win money from dishonest ways, the universe would shut down my psychic abilities, and this would not work, otherwise there would be a lot of rich psychics around!

This brings me on to universal laws, like I say when you are accessing the field of consciousness of everything that ever has been/is, this is a divine space. There is no room for trickery or parlour games. I always approach such matters with the respect it deserves. For example, lets say I was out with friends enjoying a celebratory glass of wine and someone asked me to "tune in" or give them a reading, the answer is always no. I would not enter into the divine space after drinking alcohol, for one it would be disrespectful to my guides and helpers, number two, alcohol can reduce the vibration, so would make the connection less effective, number three copious amounts of alcohol can make one susceptible to lower entity attachments, so you would be likely to channel beings that have nefarious intentions. There are always respectful parameters around spiritual practices, yes we don't enter into the duality of lesser/better, but we still hold a respect for the divine space. Anyone misusing their spiritual gifts will soon have them take away, it is the universal law, simple as that.

Psychometry - Another exercise you can do to develop your psychic skills, is what is known as psychometry. Just like we can programme crystals to hold a certain frequency, normal everyday animate objects will also hold with them energies of the place they are in, or the people who are near by. Psychometry is the act of tuning into an object, then seeing what impressions and energies you can pick up from them. An easy way to begin with is with jewellery, because jewellery is worn close to the body, and is often made from gold/silver/gem stones that are good conductors of energy, these items can capture the essence of the energetic field of the wearer.

Ideally you would do this exercise with a friend. Your friend would present you with a piece of jewellery that you know absolutely nothing about it's origins, or owner, lets say they present with their grandmother's wedding ring. They would not tell you it was their grandmother's ring, you would just take the item, and open your heart to allow any impressions or visions, to come through. If your gift was clairaudience you might hear words, if you are clairvoyant you might see pictures, if you are clairsentient you might just feel, claircognizant you might just know about the object.

Don't try to think or intellectualize this process, just allow it to unfold naturally. Also don't try to make something fit a narrative or paradigm that you think might be acceptable. When we first start to open up to the spiritual realm, often people will not be sure if they are just imagining what they get, it is very common when first starting out to doubt yourself. My advice around this would be just say what you see, don't be shy, remember any new skill takes some practice. Ideally you would be doing this exercise with a friend who was encouraging and supportive, be light-hearted about it. One thing about jewellery, it will hold the energy frequency of whom ever has worn it previously. If your grandmother's wedding ring had been passed on to your grandmother from her aunty, you may well be tuning into the aunty's frequency, so be kind to yourself when receiving feedback from others about your reading.

Due to the residual energy, I personally do not like to buy or wear antique jewellery, because I can feel the energy of the previous owners. A personal story I have around every day objects holding energy frequencies is this; several years ago we were renovating our home, we were looking for some doors that would be in keeping with the style of the old house. We bought a couple of internal second-hand wooden doors off E-bay. When I came to sand down the doors and re-paint them, I felt an awful foreboding energy, without even thinking about it, I could see and sense that the doors had witnessed domestic abuse, and violence, the wooden doors were holding this in their energy field. Luckily we had stored the doors in the garage, so I had not invited this energy into my home. Obviously I did not want this energy in my home, so I did a little ceremony where I cleansed the doors with sage smoke, sent light to the situation, and especially to the people involved, then asked that the energy of the doors be returned to the original frequency of the wood. The negative energy had been dispersed, so I was able to carry on sanding them down and painting them as normal.

This is an example of how we can maintain the frequency of the space around us, but as said previously, we need to first be in the position to be able to recognise and decode the energy in the first place, and that is where this spiritual development comes in handy. The more in tune with the field you get, the more able you will be to deal with such things. The key to developing any new skill, or enhancing any talent is practice, practice, practice.

Photo readings - Another fun way of expanding our psychic awareness is doing photo readings. Again, ideally this would be done with a friend. They would give you a photo of someone you don't know, and you would go through the same process of tuning into the energy of the person, then seeing what impressions you might get about that person. If you are new to all of this, I will give an example of the typical things that you might get from a photo. Lets pretend I'd been presented with a black and white photo of a young woman, in a summer dress and cardigan. I might typically give this sort of feedback to the enquirer:-

"I sense this lady was very fun loving, and had a very good sense of humour. (clairsentience), she is telling me that she used to work in a bakery (clairaudience), she's saying the job was hard work, and I am feeling an ache in my body (clairsentience) but she says she used to have a lot of fun at work when the boss was out of the way (clairaudience). She's showing me her home now, I can see she lived in a terraced house, made from red bricks (clairvoyance), she kept the house very neat and tidy, but the house is very busy, lots of people coming and going, lots of children. She's telling me they were her sister's children, she says she never wanted to get married, and says she was pressured all the time, but it wasn't for her, so she lived with her sister's family, (clairaudience)".

The reading might go on with details such as this, at some point I would usually ask the person if they have any message for the enquirer. It might go something like this:-

"The lady (who I think is on the vibration of a great aunt) is saying that you are in a situation where someone is putting pressure on you to do something you don't feel in your heart is right to do. This lady is saying to hold firm to your own wishes and wants, and is reminding you that it is your life, and you make your own sovereign choices".

The above example uses a variety of methods, ie. clairvoyance, clairaudience and clairsentience, and to reach that level of reading may require some degree of development. However, it is an example of the types of things you may come across when tuning in. For example, you get a feel for the character of the person, as well as their work and personal life. There are no hard and fast rules when reading an object or a photograph, the main thing is to trust your impressions, don't over-think and intellectualize it, and don't take it too seriously. No one gets it 100% right all the time, even experienced readers.

Flower readings - A lovely gentle way to give someone a reading is to use a flower. Ask them to bring a flower to you, it can be from the garden, grass verge or shop brought, the flower will represent the enquirer. Hold the flower, observe it, and tune into it. How does it feel? Can you feel any emotion with it, ie. happy, sad, nervous, bold, timid? Does the flower look fresh and vital? Or does it feel limp and tired? Was the stem cut neatly? Or are was it torn from the plant? You may be able to glean the emotional state of the enquirer through the medium of the flower. There are other clues you can go on as well, for example, often the way the flower is at the stem, i.e where it left the plant, can denote the birth of the enquirer. If the base of the flower stem is smooth, then chances are the person's birth was smooth, it it looks torn and damaged, a more tricky birth is indicated. You can use the flower for clues about the enquirer, the petals could represent children or family members, if you are sensitive to colours, you may get impressions from the hue and scent of the flower. It is just about using the vibration of the flower, as a tool to tune into the enquirer's energy field.

Guess the object/person - This is a fun game that children love to play. Lay a number of everyday items on a tray, for example, a button, some scissors, a spoon, a crystal, a tennis ball etc, at least ten items, take a good look at the tray of objects. Either use a blindfold, or simply turn your back on your friend, whilst your friend chooses one of the objects, ask them to concentrate on the object they have chosen, then try to guess which of the everyday objects they have chosen. Same as the other exercises, don't overthink it. Often the first thing that comes to mind will be the right one. You can also use a pack of playing cards to do this, ask your friend to pick a card, and concentrate on it, then try to guess which one they picked.

Another game children love to play, is guess the person. This works really well if there are several people taking part. A volunteer sits on a chair, and covers their eyes with a blindfold. One person steps forward near to the chair, whilst the others take a step back. The volunteer on the chair tries to guess who the person is near to the chair, they do this by tuning into the person's auric field, and feeling their energy. Again the purpose of this exercise is to practice tuning into someone's auric field, and getting a feel for their energies. In terms of the ethics around this, once you have developed your psychic skills, you would not go around tuning into someone's auric field, just to have a nosey, that would be contrary to the universal law. It comes down to our old friend consent, you need to gain someone's explicit consent, before tuning into their energy field. If they have asked you to read their energy, that's fine, but just as you would not let yourself into someone's home uninvited, just to have a snoop, in the same way, you would not go into someone's energy field just to have a nosey. If you did, you would soon have your psychic abilities shut down by your guides and helpers.

Psychic Writing/Automatic Writing - Psychic writing and automatic writing are the same thing. It is where you invite spirits to channel through you via your pen/pencil and paper. Like everything else, it is very important to open a sacred space whilst engaging with this, and therefore, only inviting in the entities with the highest and best intention for all concerned. Often, I find that spirit like to work with pencil as opposed to pens. I would get a blank sheet of paper, then just ask if there is anything that wants to be channelled through. I may find myself doodling, and on other occasions I have written in a beautiful script type font, when actually my own hand writing is terrible!. Sometimes it seems like a random collection of scribble that's difficult to decipher, other times I've had names and sentences given. Personally I've not tried automatic writing for several years, but if this is something that you feel drawn to, keep practising, like everything else it takes time for a skill to be mastered, the more you practice it, the stronger your connection with your spirit team will become.

Psychic Art - Working with the same methods as psychic writing, in psychic art, spirit channel through you to create a picture. Again, open with putting in place a sacred space, then allow spirit to guide your hand. Some mediums call themselves psychic artists, they will channel the spirit of a loved one, then produce a picture of them. Some people report to be poor at drawing in their "normal" life, but are able to draw and paint via psychic art. Again, this is not a method that is a favourite of mine, but I have a friend who channels spirit through her art, and uses the colours she brings through to heal, how wonderful. Why not give it a go, if you feel attracted to this method.

YOUR INDIVIDUAL EFFORTS MAKE A DIFFERENCE

I've stated previously that with regard to spiritual development, it is not a race or an ego-centred point scoring exercise. Each and everyone of us are born spiritual, it is our divine birth right, we all have the divine creator life spark within us. Since the fall of Atlantis, in this latest cycle of human existence, the way our societies have been structured have been to deliberately divorce us from our spiritual natures. This has been from many different sources.

I have spoken about the war on our frequencies, but things like our modern day living arrangements, where community living is scarce, and many people live alone, and feel isolated, the wage-slave life of working 40 hours plus, to barely be able to afford a roof over our heads and food in our stomach, this is to keep us in the rat-race, our focus merely on survival, so we don't have time to think, be creative, and turn our attention to our spiritual selves. Also instead of being a place where natural talents are encouraged and developed, the educational system is little more than a propaganda indoctrination centre, where minions are churned out repeating the mainstream narrative.

A further example of the war on our frequencies is the medical system, which is designed to keep us dependant on big pharma, and is not really created to heal or help anyone. All of this, and many more things not mentioned here, have specifically been designed to prevent us from stepping into our divine power. But the good news is that their plan isn't working. As astrologically we are receiving upgrades and light codes daily, resulting in more and more people waking up to their spiritual natures. I think this is wonderful! 30 years ago, before the internet and Youtube, before spiritual books were available in ordinary bookshops, this path was quite a lonely place to be. I love the fact that now it is easy to connect with like-minded people, and information is available everywhere. As more people wake up, it encourages others to open up to their spiritual selves too, and as a collective we are a huge force of light, surging through the planet.

No matter where you are on your spiritual journey, remember, it takes trillions of individual droplets of water to make an ocean, so each step forward you make, is a victory for everyone, another drop added to the vast ocean of light. No spiritual effort is ever wasted, and everyone's effort is as valuable and important as the next person's. We all have our own path to walk, our own soul contract. Just because you don't have a public profile on the internet, doesn't mean that your work isn't vital and valuable, because it is!

I would like to extend a message from the universe, from the Great Spirit, Divine Light of Source,

"Thank you all for your determination and effort, we see it all, every private intention for the light, every whisper of gratitude, every healing thought. Your individual efforts add to the great golden pool of love that is accumulating on your etheric fields. Never underestimate your power, and the effect it has on the universe when you send forth, from your heart, pure love. Always remember, we are with you every step of the way, encouraging you and cheering you on from the wings, all you need to do is think of us, and call to us, and we are here."

Whenever I have channelled messages from the higher realms, they are always very encouraging and thankful for all our efforts. Make no mistake being human at this juncture is not for the faint hearted, nevertheless we all chose to be here for these end times (end times of 3D world). These times are literally biblical, and lets be honest the more awake we have been to the truth of what's really been going on, the harder it has been. We have chosen to see uncomfortable truths, rather than comforting lies, it would have been far easier to remain sound asleep, oblivious to what's really going on.

Chances are if you are listening to this, or reading this work, then on some level you will be a healer, or a great holder of the light. Pretty soon, we will all be stepping into our divine roles, to help those who are only just waking up to the truth. The stronger your connection to the divine, or the more confidence you have in your spiritual abilities, the easier the journey is. A bit like a sportsman, when you begin training, you get out of breath and your muscles hurt, but after regular, repeated practice, it becomes much easier and more natural. Therefore, I encourage you all to regularly and repeatedly practice the exercises given here, and remember, no effort is wasted, where we go one we go all.

CLOSING DOWN THE SACRED SPACE

Once we have finished our spiritual practice, it is important that we specifically intend to close down the sacred space. This can be with a quick and simple prayer. A typical example might be

"Great Spirit, Divine Creator of Source, we give thanks for all we have received today. We thank all those in the spirit world that have assisted in today's proceedings. May we continue to receive your wisdom and love, and ask that we take this love and wisdom out into our daily lives to help inspire others. Also, thank you for assisting in the healing we have sent out today, and please can you keep this healing light going for as long as necessary. Thanks again Great Spirit, until we meet again. Amen"

CHAPTER 3
EXTENDING YOUR SPIRITUAL PRACTICE

Now that you have developed a good routine for daily spiritual practice, lets now consider what else we can do, to enhance our connection to the Great Spirit. The more our vibrational level increases, the more inclined we will be for service to others, it is consistent with the natural laws, as we receive so shall we give. Like a flow of energy, constantly circulating, ebb and flow, give and take. The 5D paradigm is all about energy exchange, to keep in balance and alignment, we need to give as well as take. If we receive spiritual gifts from the universe, we will naturally want to use these gifts in service to all. It is this philosophy that has driven my earth healing grid work, as well as my therapeutic services. Here is a short poem I wrote in 2016, that encapsulates the 5D life.

Mid-Summer Thoughts

Sending out the Love
Giving out the light
Never getting weary
Of working for the right

Mother Earth the focus
Of this trip, my path
Thoughts and energies evolving
As Mother Earth's revolving

Restore, Refresh, Re-energise
Illuminate the way
Light traversing ley lines
Of a never-setting day

RESTORE, REFRESH RE-ENERGISE!

Since 2013 I have been focussed on specifically bringing in the light from the universe, and anchoring it into the planet. My mission has been to assist the ascension process, by switching up the vibrational level of our wonderful mother earth. I've been mindfully bringing in the light from the seven suns that are available to us now, along with energy from my home planet Rycia. This has taken many forms, from simply imagining it anchoring into the land around my home, extending to other places I visit whilst on holidays (vacations) and days out, as well as sacred sites and ley lines. Lately I have been asked to send out energy to remote locations all over the world. Intention is everything, there are no constraints when it comes to energy directing, a thought is an action in the 5D realm.

Another significant part of my role is energy clearing work, again, this is extremely varied, I never know where the universe will take me, or what or with whom I will be working with. I have my own regular team on the etheric realms, which include my Dragons, Archangel Michael, and Archangel Raphael, along with my family of higher Galactics. But then each place I clear, will lend itself to whoever is the most suitable person for the job. For example, often when I clear ancient sites or Trig points, Ascended Master Merlin shows up. When I do clearing involving children and the DUMBS Commander Ashtar often gets involved. Whilst clearing a stone Circle in the Lake District in England I met with a massive ship full of benign Acturians, then whilst in Spain clearing a reptilian infested church Ascended Masters Jesus, and Lady Nadia helped. My role in this is to be the organic human being incarnated on the earth, with the free will to ask for the appropriate help. They use my free will, and the high vibe portal that I create with my body, that enables them to step down and do the work. As seen from a 5D perspective, this is actually quite a simple process, after all, everything is about energy and frequency, so if I am able to create a suitable portal for them, using my own vibrational code, the rest will follow, I trust them, and leave them to it. I never feel fear whilst doing this work, because there is no fear in the 5th dimension or higher, I have complete trust in the divine wisdom of the Great Spirit.

Everyone has the ability to bring in and anchor light on the planet, you may already have your own method of doing this, one thing to remember is that everything is about intention. Lets say you had seen that some people in your on-line community were going to do a ley line clearing in say Denmark, if you wanted to add your energy to that, you don't need to know the precise details, you can literally just set your intention that you are adding your energy to the grid work in Denmark, as mentioned by the online community. That is enough, you have set a clear intention, and clearly directed the energy to that place, the universe will do the logistics for you!

If you are new to this, and would like some guidance on how to do your own energy clearing work, here is my meditation guide;

RESTORE, REFRESH, RE-ENERGISE MEDITATION GUIDE
INVOCATION/PROTECTION

Take some deep breaths, put aside all the cares of the day. Take some more deep breaths, connect yourself, to yourself in this moment. Call in Archangel Michael, and your team of helpers, for me that would be the dragons, the unicorns, the higher Galactic's, and Archangel Raphael, I'm also calling in the ancestors of this place, the spirits of this place, the elementals of this place.

As I call these in, I am making it very clear, that I am only calling those in with the highest and best intention for all concerned. The highest and the best for everyone. We know now that we have the protection of the Archangels and all those mentioned, and they are coming in on the vibration to serve the highest and best for humanity and all concerned.

ACTIVATE YOUR CRYSTAL

Take a crystal or stone, ask that your crystal is set to a 5th dimensional energy space or higher. Set the intention that your crystal will be vibrating at 5D or higher at all times. Take a moment to link with that, and the intend that your crystal now links to all of us, all over the world that are taking part in the Restore, Refresh Re-energise practice. So now your crystal is linked to my crystal, and everyone else's crystal. We have now created a beautiful, powerful grid of 5th dimensional energy (or higher), worldwide, between each other. Now set the intention to link our energy grid, to all the crystals all over the world that are still embedded in the earth, and all the unloved, unused crystals, we are sending our love, and creating a massive grid of high dimensional energy, and a framework of energy pathways all around the globe. See them as beautiful, golden pulsating energy lines.

SET THE INTENTION

Repeat out loud 3 times (or in your head if not suitable to say out loud)

"I command that we receive the relevant light keys and codes to accelerate the earth's ascension" (say this 3 times)

OPEN YOUR OWN PERSONAL PORTAL
VIA YOUR 12 CHAKRA SYSTEM

Starting with your Earth Star Chakra beneath the souls of your feet, imagine and intend that opening up, then moving up, through your body intend that the others open up and activate. We have the base, the sacrel, the navel, the solar plexus, the radiant golden heart, the throat, the third eye, the crown. The causal chakra, which is located behind your head, the soul star several metres above your head, then finally the stellar gateway, which is connected to your home planet.

RESTORE, REFRESH, RE-ENERGISE

Now we are ready for the three R's. We are going to imagine and intend the light to come from the universe, the source your home planet, imagine and intend the light coming in via your chakras, passing through your body, and anchoring it into planet earth. We are bringing in that high energy, and are repeating RRR 3x3;

"Restore, Refresh, Re-energise"
"Restore, Refresh, Re-energise"
"Restore, Refresh, Re-energise"   *x3*

Know that this powerful mantra is making a real difference to the frequency of the planet, and the energy pathways of the earth. Imagine all the energy meeting up with others doing the same, joining in a high frequency community. You are never alone in this practice, we are one, can you feel this in your soul?

CELEBRATE JOY AND ABUNDANCE, FEEL THE GRATITUDE

We are now adding joy, abundance and gratitude to this practice, with another mantra said 3x3

"We are stronger, we are brighter, we are lighter"
"We are stronger, we are brighter, we are lighter"
"We are stronger, we are brighter, we are lighter".........x3

Feel the love, joy and fun, feel the gratitude for this practice.

GIVE THANKS, CLOSE THE SPACE

We thank all those who have taken part in this practice, we thank Archangel Michael, the angels and Archangels, the Dragons, our own healing teams, the ancestors of this place, the spirits and elementals of this place, the higher Galactic's, we thank everyone who has taken part in this service. We can feel the love, joy and abundance, and we know this has made a huge difference to the energy and frequency of the entire planet, and that will impact on the entire cosmos.

Thank you, Thank you, Thank you.
It is done, It is done, It is done.

GOOD SPIRITUAL HYGIENE

In the 5D realm, looking after ones spiritual hygiene, is as natural as looking after ones physical hygiene, but how much attention does the average person, living in the 3D, give to spiritual hygiene? In the 3D world we may choose to look after our bodies, nourishing them with food, taking appropriate exercise and rest, bathing and grooming to keep our bodies in good shape, but rarely would one consider spiritual hygiene, as we have been conditioned by the cultural norms imposed by the former controllers to not see this as important. However, the more attuned to 5D we become, the more relevant this will seem, to the point where it becomes a vital part of our daily routine.

Here is an example of some of the things I incorporate into my daily routine, that helps me to keep in the highest vibration possible.

Gratitude – As mentioned before, 5D living is all about energy exchange, a constant, vital flow of energy. Showing gratitude is an important way of maintaining this energy flow, as it opens up space within your heart for new levels of love and abundance to flow through. Upon awakening, I start my day thanking the Great Spirit for all I have received. Even if life isn't rosy, and even when I am experiencing difficulties, I will still thank the Great Spirit for those experiences, as I know that it's been the difficulties in my life that have enabled me to develop strength and resilience. When life feels good, it's easy to give thanks for all the good things, such as relationships, the glorious abundance of nature, sunny days, holidays etc.

Setting the Intention for the day – Next I would specifically set a clear intention for the day, we need to do this, so that the universe knows exactly what we want. Think of it this way, lets say you go to a restaurant and say to the waiter you wish to order food, the waiter needs to know what sort of food you desire, otherwise you might end up with a dish not to your taste, even though it was what you ordered....food! Be specific with your intention, then you will more likely manifest the outcome. For example, I might say, "Great Spirit, please help me to stay in 5D vibration or higher at all times today. Please let my connection to spirit grow ever stronger and brighter, please help me to help others on their journey, and help me to fulfil my earthly mission, I also do not consent to being abducted". I always add the bit about not consenting to being abducted, simply because I don't consent and need to make that crystal clear!..Due to my energy codes, I would be of interest to negative ET's, I experienced an abduction in my 20's (a story for another day). It is vital that we all specifically state if we do not consent to something, because if we don't then sometimes implied consent is taken, i.e if you have not stated NO then the bad guys will take that as consent. Even the bad guys are governed by universal law, which denotes that consent must be given, so if you state you do not consent, and they go against that, then they will have to face the karmic consequences of breaking universal law.

Bless your food and water – I love to have a cup of coffee first thing in the morning, some may judge this as a 3D habit, but I don't care, I enjoy coffee, so I'm not going to deny myself this human pleasure. What I do though, is bless the water I use to make the coffee. Here in the UK, currently they are adding fluoride and any number of heavy metals into our tap water, in an attempt to lower our frequency. Therefore, I have bought a Berkey water filter, with added fluoride filters in an attempt to purify the water I drink.

However, the single most important thing I can do, is bless the water and set the frequency of the water, when I pour it into the filter. Just like crystals, we can alter the frequency of water, by setting our intention towards it. Originally our waters were crystal clear, pure and brilliant, with a frequency of 5D or higher, this is what was intended for our consumption. Like everything else, this has been altered, but the good news is that each and every one of us has the power to re-programme the water we drink. It's easy, all you need to do is specifically set the intention and say something like this; "I bless this water, and ask that it's frequency is set to 5D or higher", simple as that, you now have high vibe water, which will have a positive impact on the cells in your body.

If I have the good fortune to go wild swimming in the ocean, lake or river, I will speak to the water elementals, thank them for their service, then I will programme all the water in that space, and linking to those water ways, to a frequency of 5D or higher at all times, and ask that the waters are returned to the intended frequency by the Great Spirit. Doing this, adds to the 5D vibration of the planet, and is assisting the collective planetary energetic upgrade, you can even do this at your local swimming pool, so why not give it a try next time you go swimming or paddling?

On a side note, when I'm in the ocean, and I've programmed the waters, I often call to the cetaceans (whales and dolphins), thank them for their tremendous service, of helping to keep the frequencies of the oceans in tact, I also thank them for being the keepers of the knowledge from the Atlantean ages, they have really helped planet earth's energy codes, more than we realise, so I honour this, send out my love and gratitude, and communicate to them from my heart. The result of this, is that I see a disproportionate amount of whales and dolphins. I was once doing this on the East coast of England, and saw two pods of dolphins. I was speaking to a lady who had lived there for 70 years, she said she had only ever seen one dolphin there in her entire life, she couldn't believe what she saw that afternoon. Perhaps I should have told her what I had been doing, and the reason they had showed up!

Bless your food – Just as we can programme the frequency of water, we can do the same for our food. Even if we are working towards self-sufficiency by growing our own food etc, the reality of things is that many of us are still having to rely on mass produced food, that may have lost it's life-force and vitality. It is the life-force and vitality of food that truly nourishes our bodies. We all know that fresh vegetables and fruit eaten directly from the garden tastes like no other, and gives us an extra sense of satisfaction. This is because the life-force, the living aura of the food is still there when we consume it, not to mention that it will have been produced with love, and without the chemicals of commercially grown food. Whilst we are still in the transition between 3D and 5D and are still eating commercially produced food, we can help ourselves by mindfully setting the intention of our food. For example, we may say something like this "I bless this meal, and set it's frequency to 5D or higher, I give thanks to the people who have helped to produce this food". Simple as that, this little intention will help negate the effects of any chemicals/processing, and is on the vibration of gratitude, which is abundance consciousness.

Conscious Awareness – In the old paradigm, spirituality was often tied to religion, with many religions taking a specific day for worship. For example, in the Christian faith, Sundays was the day deemed for spiritual matters, do as you like all week, then as long as you attend church every Sunday, and ask a priest for forgiveness, you'd be ok. Or in the new age world, spirituality took on setting specific time aside for "spiritual matters", sitting on yoga mats, attending workshops, meditation etc, in a time and space separate from day-to-day life.

In 5D consciousness, spiritual practice is weaved into the very fabric of day-to-day life. You cannot have one without the other. We would start our day as mentioned above, with gratitude, setting an intention for the day, blessing our food and water, so what else? It's about having a constant awareness and connection to the Great Spirit, you are always spiritually online so to speak, not just on Sundays or when at workshops. When you are out and about, you would be tuned into nature, seeing little signs and signals. For example, if I'm going about my daily routine, if a bird crosses my path, I will thank the bird for being there, tell it I love it. If a tree catches my eye, I will thank it for it's great service, and send it my love. If an insect flies past, I will shout out a greeting. If I see a horse, I will send it unicorn blessings. A constant atunement to the energy space around me. Where we go one we go all, we are all united sharing this energetic space, I am the birds the bees, the trees, and they are me in unity consciousness. It is seeing ourselves as separate that gives the polarity of 3D, in 5D we are one as multidimensional creator beings, made in the image of God, our potentials are endless.

In 5D, we have a constant connection to our higher selves, we allow ourselves to be consciously guided by it. For example, lets say I was involved in a minor car accident, or I fell off my bicycle, I would instantly look at the reason I had invited this into my life, and look for the soul lesson my higher self was wanting me to experience. In 3D, we would view these things as "bad luck", when the reality of it is that we are the conscious creators of our life, we just need to look at things from a higher perspective.

In 5D consciousness, we would be consciously aware of our thoughts and emotions. Experiencing emotions is what makes us human. Some extra-terrestrial races (ET's), such as reptilians do not have the emotional component, they are unable to feel any emotion. In current psychiatry, it is known that around 1% of the population are classed as psychopaths, i.e devoid of any capability to feel emotion or empathy for others. I believe this 1% of the population are the hybrid reptilians, the shapeshifting reptiles, that pretend to be human. To me, this would make total sense, as interestingly, it is also 1% of the population that made up the elite class. A very popular song, sang at the freedom rallies I attended along with hundreds of thousands of other truthers in London in 2021, was the song "we are the 99%......you can stick your poison vaccine up your arse!"

Indeed we are the 99%, and every organic human can feel emotion, and has the capacity to feel empathy for others. In the 3D world, often we let our emotions govern us, we may be addicted to drama, and may sit with maudlin emotions for long periods of time, which will inevitably have the effect of lowering our vibration. In the 5D world, we would be very aware when emotions arise, we would acknowledge the emotion, experience and learn from it, then we would let it go and move on, thus keeping our vibration in tact.

Lets now compare a scenario, looking it at it first from 3D consciousness, then compare the same situation looking at it from a 5D perspective. Jenny has been invited for a night out with her work friends, these particular friends have a tendency to bitch and bully another colleague, Jenny doesn't always feel comfortable about this, but she wants to fit in, and avoid confrontation, so she accepts the invite. Jenny knows that a large part of the evening will be spent bitching about the other colleague. As she is getting ready for the evening out, she slips down the stairs, and feels acute pain in her ankle. She gets her partner to take her to the emergency department of the hospital. In the 3D world, whilst waiting to be seen at the hospital she would post on all her social medias "oh my god, I'm sitting in the A&E (ER) department, in so much pain....." This would elicit much attention, and drama from her 3D friends. Jenny would love the attention of everyone commenting, and asking if she was ok. After being discharged with a sprained ankle, she would post pictures of her swollen ankle, then would spend the evening feeling sorry for herself that she had missed out on the evening out, but on the other hand she would really enjoy seeing all the dramatic posts from her friends, regarding her ankle, as this would inflate her 3D ego, and give a sense of importance. Other than feeling as though she had bad luck, and things like that always happen to her, once the attention on social media had stopped, Jenny would give little thought to the matter. Now, from a 5D perspective, as soon as Jenny slipped down the stairs, her first thought would be "why have I made myself slip on the stairs? What does my higher-self and the universe want me to learn?". This may then facilitate her contemplation of the dynamic with the work colleagues. She would then see that her going along with the bullying of the other colleague was not consistent with her values, and joining them for a night out would only add her energy to this unhealthy situation. From a 5D perspective, Jenny would be stoic about the pain she was experiencing in her ankle, and might attribute this to experiencing karma for the unkind things she herself had said about the colleague. She would see the pain as a message, acknowledge it, then let it go. She may then thank the universe for bringing about this situation, that has enabled her to learn a valuable lesson, and resolve to energetically separate herself from the bullies. She may then contact a healer friend, and ask her to energetically look at her ankle or may use her own psychic abilities to determine the status of her ankle to see if it needed any treatment. She may then ask the universe to take away the pain, thanking it for the experience, but saying now she has learned her lesson, the pain was no longer necessary. Two very different responses, to the same situation.

So getting back to emotions, it is very human to experience a range of emotions, it is our emotions that enable us to love others, and feel connected and bonded with others, it is also our emotions that enable us to feel sadness and despair. The key to healthy emotions is to let them arise naturally, acknowledge they are there, look at what they are telling you, learn from them, then LET THEM GO. I'm not saying let go the emotion of love, it is wonderful to stay in a constant loving vibration, but I am saying don't sit maudlin over difficult emotions such as sadness, despair, anxiety, look for the message then move on, focus your attention on something else.

Being your Authentic Self – In 5D, there is very little space for fakeness, as everyone will be able to see clearly your energy field, including your truth and intentions. On the other hand, in 3D, it is easy to put out a fake persona, and to outwardly project one reality, when in reality you are thinking and feeling something else. I have always had the ability to see straight through people, and been able to naturally discern the truth of someone's energy field. Countless times during my life, I have discerned the wolf in sheep's clothing so to speak, and have found it impossible to behave in a fake manner towards a wolf that everyone else believes is a sheep, this has not always made me popular. However, since truth always comes out in the end, time after time the wolf has been revealed, and I have been vindicated. Many of us who discerned the fake convid vaccine will know how that feels!

I have always spoken from my heart, and spoken my truth, and I personally can't wait until I am in a realm where everyone can see my true self and my true intention, as I know in my heart that I am a good person, who truly only wants the best for everyone, I would welcome everyone seeing the real me, as like so many of you reading this, we have been misunderstood for speaking our truth.

If you are at all worried about the fact that in 5D, everyone will be able to see clearly your energy code, and the real you, then that would indicate that you still have some unhealed parts of yourself that you need to integrate. Be gentle with yourself, ask the universe and your higher-self for guidance for the best way of helping yourself with this, for example taking some 5D therapy may be a good idea.

Discernment - has been a huge lesson for humanity during recent years, I think this has been in preparation for us moving to 5D. We need to get used to seeing things clearly. We need to let go of our 3D ego selves, and be prepared to see the truth, in all matters, even things that are not pleasant or pretty. It is misguided to think that to be spiritual, one only has to see the good in people, the reality of it is, there is evil in this 3D world, good and bad, light and dark, yin and yang. Think of the horrific reality of human and child trafficking, the demonic adrenochrome and organ harvesting facilities, as well as the reality that reptilians see human's merely as useless eaters and a food source, they see us as meat they can eat! Difficult as this is, we need to acknowledge this, understand that this happened, so that we never allow it to happen again.

The higher your vibration rises, the easier it will be to naturally discern the truth. The eagle sours high above the mountains, it's elevated status gives it the perfect birds eye view, it can see exactly what's going on, for miles around. On the other hand, the earth-bound lizard can only see it's immediate surroundings, it is unable to see the bigger picture of the landscape, and cannot foresee what's coming next.

CHAPTER 4
MORE SPIRITUAL TRUTHS

Karma - Since we left source and took our celestial journeys, the aim has been for us to experience life in different realms, accrue enough wisdom and insight so that we can merge our consciousness back with source. We may have many different incarnations on numerous planets and planetary systems. However, it is known throughout the cosmos, that life on planet earth offers the incarnate an absolutely unique experience, because planet earth herself is completely unique. I can tell you this from my own awareness, and soul memories of life on other planets, there is no-where quite like planet earth.

There are several reasons for this, not only is planet earth placed in a position in the cosmos that leaves it open to a truly diverse range of energetic influences, enabling a vast range of animals, vegetation and minerals to evolve. But also the physicality of planet Earth enables incarnates to experience life in a unique way. Furthermore, the human race is the master race throughout the cosmos, made in the image of God. In addition, planet Earth is the living library of all of creation, and as organic humans, once we have fully activated our DNA we have the potential to unlock the library doors so to speak. Coupled with all of that, organic humans have the latent potential to be gods, we have the codes written in our DNA, even though most of our DNA is dormant currently.

We have been having these experiences on this unique planet, with the highest potentials possible, so if the aim of our celestial journey is to learn our lessons, perfect our being so that we may return to source, planet earth has provided us with the perfect classroom.

The process or modus operandi that has allowed us to learn the necessary lessons, is karma and our soul contracts. Prior to birth, we make our soul contracts, we have a time to be born and a time to die, we plan the main lessons we wish to learn, and our higher-self and earth star chakra will create circumstances that give us opportunities to learn our soul lessons, this is just the plan though, we have free will and can decide whether or not we stick to the plan. Often, the more lessons we have chosen to learn in an incarnation, the more difficult this will be. A major determinate in our life plans will be the status of our karma. If we have gone off track in a previous life and caused harm to someone in some way, then we will have a karmic debt to pay, i.e we will need to experience the pain we caused the person in a previous life. I would add here that there is no vengeful god forcing us to experience our karma, we will eventually choose to do so, as learning our lessons is our way to enlightenment.

In 3D our karma is in equal measures, you get back what you give, this is where I believe the expressions in the bible "an eye for an eye" or "reap what you sow" comes from. You do good you get the positive consequences; you do bad you get it back in equal measure. However, in 5D karma is tenfold. If you do a good or bad deed, you will get the karma x10, a tangible reward for good effort, but a marked deterrent for deeds not akin to 5D, a clever universal law that keeps everyone incentivised to keep their frequency high, and keep progressing spiritually. Another thing to add here is that in 3D karma can take life-times to ripen, but in 5D karma is pretty instant.

Death and Dying – Most modern western cultures have a very unhealthy, and unnatural approach to death and dying. I would go as far as to say that death is a taboo subject, not to be mentioned or alluded to, just in case by doing so somehow brings the dreaded event closer. Our cultures have programmed us to fear death, and even worse, many have lead us to truly believe that once you die, that is it, the end, curtains. Of course, if you are a non player character (NPC), then true, you have no soul to move on, but if you are an organic human being, each incarnation is just a brief moment, a soul having a human experience.

When viewed from this perspective, life all of a sudden doesn't seem so serious or important. Remember, the dark forces want us to live in fear because we are easier to control and manipulate when we are in the fear vibration, therefore they have propagated this skewed viewpoint on death, so they can remain in control. Once the masses are aware that we are multi dimensional beings, merely having a human experience, it would be game over for that lot. So we are taught to fear death, fear going to hell, fear living in purgatory, the religions have been the conduit for the death propaganda.

Many indigenous cultures, including the native American cultures, saw death in the context of the cycle of life. Sometimes if the elders knew that their time on earth was drawing to a close, they would remove themselves from the tribe, and go up to the mountains to die naturally, a complete cycle. Upon their death their bodies would be taken by the animals, or returned to nature.

I've always found the concept of gravestones, and keeping artificial flowers like shrines a bit creepy and unnecessary. I don't buy cut flowers for people in the spirit world, I would rather plant a tree to honour their life, and then enjoy the seasons of the tree in their memory.

Here is a poem I wrote about death in 1994.

Over the Rainbow

Well it's one for all beyond that crest
It's not the end when laid to rest
We live full lives just like before
In the spirit world beyond that door

We merely loose our physical form
Our mind and thoughts are all re-born
All the good or bad that we've done here
Determine where we go in the spirit sphere

The spirit world is a much fairer place
With no discrimination twix station or race
Power is not placed on material wealth or possession
But determined by love, truth, our own progression

So if we bear these thoughts in mind
We should always endeavour to be true and kind
Though often difficult on this earth plane
In spirit the rewards we are certain to gain

If we want to be free from fear, it's time we re-evaluated our stance on death and dying. I am not saying that losing a loved one isn't gut wrenchingly difficult, I'm not saying that if we see things from a spiritual stance then losing a loved one will be easy to navigate, of course it won't. We will still feel the raw and desperate loss associated with it. But if we have a knowing that there is a time to live and a time to die, and see a life as a brief human experience in the context of eternity, then it is so much easier to cope with when we do lose someone special.

Reincarnation – I have had the good fortune, or should I say more accurately, the spiritual insight to have spontaneously seen into some of my past lives. I write a chapter on this in my first book, Enchanted Earth. I know that I have had hundreds, if not thousands of lives on earth (and other realms), in various different forms. I have spontaneously seen myself leaving lifetimes, undertaking my life review, then choosing to re-incarnate again. With this inner knowledge, I find it impossible to fear death like others might. I can also see that I chose to incarnate into circumstances that will benefit my soul learning. When we view our existence from this perspective, we let go of any notion of blaming others for our rubbish lives, and realise that we are truly the creators of our life, stepping fully into personal responsibility.

Take my current life as Gillian England, I chose to have very difficult circumstances in my early years. My childhood was very unhappy, I received constant negative appraisal, perpetual negative messages about myself. This in fact was a gift, as it enabled me to develop a strong connection to spirt, and I knew that I was a good person in my heart and soul, even if other's couldn't see that. Fifty odd trips around the sun later, when I step into the public arena, talking about dragons, aliens, reptilians, space craft, I honestly and truly don't give a monkeys what people think about me, because my early life taught me to believe in myself, even if no one else did. My childhood also taught me equanimity, I meet the trolls and those looking up to me as a guru in equal measure. It doesn't really matter what your opinion of me is, as long as I am pure in heart and have the best intention. I'm sure that if I would have had a childhood where I was put on a pedestal, I may have let ego slip into my work, and that is the downfall of so many.

I would add a word of caution here; if exploring your past-lives it can be very tempting to get obsessed with the details of your past lives, but remember they are done and gone, there is a good reason why most people have their memories of prior incarnations wiped out. Yes we might carry forward trauma from other lives, these might manifest as phobias or "irrational" fears of things, they might benefit from exploring and healing. But in the main, there is little benefit digging and churning up old material just for the sake of it. I believe that I have access to many of my past lives naturally, because I have the sense to just observe without getting hung up on them.

Of all the incarnations I have undertaken on planet earth, I know that this one, the life you and I are living right now, is our master life-time. The one time, that will mark a significant turning point in the evolution of planet earth and indeed the cosmos. We are indeed lucky to be here, try to remember that when life feels difficult. Keep going, we are almost there!

CHAPTER 5
USING YOUR DIVINE POWER TO INFLUENCE YOUR WORLD

I am always very keen to get the message out that all of us organic human beings, incarnated on this planet have been created in God's image, and have divine magical powers. We are all creator beings, encoded in are DNA are potentials and keys and codes, that make us the most unique and powerful beings in our universe. Even the most spiritually advanced human on earth is currently using only a fraction of the DNA available, which means that we have significantly more powers and talents ready to be tapped into. Like I have mentioned previously, increasing your personal connection to spirit, will activate more of your dormant DNA, and naturally open up more spiritual gifts and talents.

But many people don't realise that even as our spiritual evolution stands today, there is so much more we can do to help create the world we want. In this chapter, I show you various techniques, meditations and protocols that you can use to empower yourself, and help you step into your divine creator selves. Remember, this knowledge is rightfully ours, in previous civilisations we used these methods daily to create the world we wanted to live in, like everything else, this knowledge has been deliberately hidden from us by the dark forces, in an attempt to control us, and keep us enslaved However; their time is up, as a collective we are shifting the power paradigm, and reclaiming our sovereign selves, as we remember our magical powers.

Take the weather for example, did you know that we have the power to influence and change the weather, and get the weather we desire? We just need to attune ourselves to the weather elementals, and re-program them. The dark forces have been doing this for decades, then blaming global warming or climate change, as a way of justifying increased tax, and further curtailment of freedoms. It is time we reclaimed our power, below is my meditation guide,

HOW TO CREATE THE WEATHER YOU WANT.
MEDITATION GUIDE

What we need to know about the Weather Elementals - The weather is governed and controlled by the weather elementals, these are living beings of consciousness, just like you and me, although they don't have the free will that we have. In view of this, they will respond to commands and instructions. The best way in which to foster good relationships with the elementals, is to love and respect them, honour their work and their essence. It's no different from your relationships with people, if you treat people with respect, you are far more likely to get them on your side, and they are far more likely to co-operate with you.

Many of you reading this will have had lived past lives where you created your own weather systems, with your thoughts and intentions. For example, most people are aware of the Native American rain dancers. Many of you will have the soul memories of this, my job is to gently help you remember, so that you may step back into your magical power, and create the weather you want. Like with so many other things, the dark forces have not wanted us to know about our magical creative selves. Make no mistake, they have been commanding the elements, and using the weather against us for a very long time, think bush fires, floods, hurricanes, designed to cause maximum disruption and bring our vibrational levels down.

Like everything else, it is time now for us organic human beings, to claim back our divine powers, and be the creator beings we were intended to be. It's time for us to work with the weather elementals and create the weather conditions we want. How many times have you layed in bed, listening to a storm, hoping that your home won't succumb to any damage? But as you are lying there, you have been conditioned to be in a passive state, hoping for the best, but having no idea that you can influence the outcome yourself.

It is really quite a simple process, we all have the power to do this for ourselves. For example, if I hear of a storm heading my way, first of all, I would reiterate the physic force-field pyramid I've already gridded round my property, then I would communicate with the elementals, thanking them and honouring them and their work. After that I would specifically send them a lot of love, and calming energy, I would imagine them becoming serene, calm, and happy. Then I would specifically ask them to pass through my property with grace and ease, imagining the winds gently traversing my property. We have all seen news reports of weather events, where there has been mass disruption, but for some reason, seemingly against all odds a single property has remained perfectly in tact. I have no doubts whatsoever, that in these circumstances, there has been some conscious divine intervention, i.e direct communication with the weather elementals. (To be clear, I am not making reference to the Direct Energy Weapons (DEW) used in Hawaii in 2023 here, I believe that was something altogether different, a nefarious activity instigated by the dark forces).

As an individual, we are very powerful, but as a collective energy, we are unstoppable. Therefore, next time we hear of a bush fire, or potential hurricane or storm, if as a collective we all tuned in and communicated with the weather elementals, we truly have the power to extinguish any bush fire, and down-grade any hurricane. They don't want us to know this, because when we do, their power games, and ability to unleash mass disruption are over, together we are stronger, we are brighter, we are lighter.......Below is my meditation guide, on how to connect with the beautiful weather elementals.

INVOCATION/PROTECTION

Take some deep breaths, put aside all the cares of the day. Take some more deep breaths, connect yourself, to yourself in this moment. Call in Archangel Michael, and your team of helpers, for me that would be the dragons, the unicorns, my ancestors the higher Galactic's, and Archangel Raphael, I am also calling in the ancestors of this place, the spirits of this place, and very importantly for this meditation, we are calling in the weather elementals and the elementals of this place.

As I call these in, I am making it very clear, that I am only calling those in with the highest and best intention for all concerned. The highest and the best for everyone. We know now that we have the protection of the Archangels and all those mentioned, and they are coming in on the vibration to serve the highest and best for humanity and all concerned.

SET THE INTENTION

Great spirit, Divine light of Source, we give our heartfelt thanks, for everything we have received so far on our journeys. Today, Great Spirit, we ask that we may link with the beautiful weather elementals, and that they will help us manifest desirable weather conditions.

COMMUNICATE DIRECTLY WITH THE ELEMENTALS

We would like to let you know that we love, honour and respect you, our dear friends the weather elementals, and from our radiant golden hearts to yours we send our love and gratitude. We ask you, dear elementals, that you will work with us today, in order for us to experience the weather we desire.

(The weather conditions you desire, may differ, depending on where you are, and what time of year it is. Remember, we are working with the elementals, it would be unrealistic to ask for hot weather, if you were in the Northern hemisphere in January! Recently I have been cloud-busting the chem trail grey clouds, so my communication has gone something like this);

Dearest friends, the elementals, thank you for all that you do. I command you dear friends, to undo any prior weather programming placed on you by those going against the natural laws, I supersede any negative commands by asking that the skies are returned to the original state as intended by the Great Spirit, and that we may experience the organic weather patterns as was intended. I ask that you dissipate the grey skies, and I can see the thick grey clouds breaking up, and dissolving into the atmosphere, transmuting the energy, leaving the skies clear blue, allowing the healing rays of the sunshine to nourish and energise all life-forms. As I am clearly intending this, and as I am seeing the clouds dissolve, I say this mantra:

Repeat out loud 3 times (or in your head if not suitable to say out loud)

"We are stronger, we are brighter, we are lighter"
"We are stronger, we are brighter, we are lighter"
"We are stronger, we are brighter, we are lighter   x3

The clearer you set the intention, the clearer you imagine your intended outcome, and the more you are in stepped into your power, the more effective you will be.

Here is an example of how you may use your intention, to calm down a weather situation, such as a storm or a bush fire;

Dearest friends, the elementals, thank you for all that you do. I command you dear friends, to undo any prior weather programming placed on you by those going against the natural laws, I supersede any negative commands by asking that the skies are returned to the original state as intended by the Great Spirit, and that we may experience the organic weather patterns as was intended. I send my love and light to you, beautiful weather elementals, and ask that you may feel this love soothing and calming you, leaving you feeling serene and at one with the natural world. As I envisage the storm/fire calming down repeat out loud 3 times (or in your head if not suitable to say out loud)

"We are stronger, we are brighter, we are lighter"
"We are stronger, we are brighter, we are lighter"
"We are stronger, we are brighter, we are lighter"   x3

You may use the same protocol, if for example you were in need of rain, you would communicate this to the elementals, and imagine a gentle rain falling on the space around you.

GIVE THANKS, CLOSE THE SPACE

We thank all those who have taken part in this practice, we give particular thanks to the weather elementals, and the guardians of the skies. We thank Archangel Michael, and the elementals of this place, we thank everyone who has taken part in this practice.

Thank you, Thank you, Thank you.
It is done, It is done, It is done.

REVERSE THE EFFECTS OF VACCINES PROTOCOL
- MEDITATION GUIDE

Absolutely everything is about frequency. Many people are now regretting having taken vaccines, including the fake covid vaccine, and are concerned about the side effects. If you are willing to step into your own personal responsibility, develop your personal connection to the Great Spirit, and rise your vibration to a level higher than the frequency range of side-effects and disease, then you can truly reverse the effects of all vaccines.

There are some other valuable protocols you can follow, and other healing modalities that are beneficial such as hyperbaric oxygen, drinking pine needle tea, med beds etc, I suggest you research these too. But ultimately everything is about frequency, and this guide is to help you step into the spiritual side of the healing, that will set the intention, and clear the energetic pathways, which will work as a stand-alone protocol, or will compliment any other healing modality you may choose.

INVOCATION/PROTECTION

Take some deep breaths, put aside all the cares of the day. Take some more deep breaths, connect yourself, to yourself in this moment. Call in Archangel Michael, and your team of helpers. For me that would be the dragons, the unicorns, my ancestors the higher Galactic's, and Archangel Raphael, you may well have your own unique team, but always call in Archangel Michael, as he offers protection.

As I call these in, I am making it very clear, that I am only calling those in with the highest and best intention for all concerned. The highest and the best for everyone. We know now that we have the protection of the Archangels and all those mentioned, and they are coming in on the vibration to serve the highest and best for humanity and all concerned.

SET THE INTENTION

Great Spirit, I am connecting with you today, with the intention of stepping into my personal responsibility, and rising above the vibration of all the vaccines I have ever taken. I forgive myself, and my parents/care givers and any others involved, and intend to clear my energy field of every vaccine and medication I have ever taken, that has not been in my highest and best interests, leaving me pure, perfect and how God intended. I am asking for assistance with this please, dear spirit team.

FORGIVENESS

Great Spirit, I now understand that many vaccines contain human DNA, from foetal cells etc. I see and honour every single soul from that original DNA, and forgive myself for this. Great Spirit, I am acknowledging all the vaccines given to us me as a child, before I was in a position to make a conscious choice about whether or not to participate. I forgive myself and my parents/ care givers for consenting to these vaccines on my behalf. For the vaccines I consented to taking myself, I acknowledge my full responsibility for these choices I forgive myself, and I let go of any self-blame.

REVOKE ANY CONSENT

Great Spirit, I return my memory to the times when I actively rolled up my sleeves to consent to having the vaccines in my body. I take my consciousness back to each and every time I participated in the administration of vaccines, including those times I cannot remember. I am clearly stating now that I revoke my consent to all of these vaccines. I am breaking any prior contracts and agreements, and supersede all of these, by withdrawing my consent to all of them. I understand that time is an illusion, and know that my consent is now withdrawn from all these vaccine procedures.

OPEN UP YOUR 12 CHAKRAS

Starting with your Earth Star Chakra beneath the souls of your feet, imagine and intend tham opening up, then moving up, through your body intending that the others open up and activate. We have the base, the sacrel, the navel, the solar plexus, the radiant golden heart, the throat, the third eye, the crown, the causal chakra, which is located behind your head, the soul star several metres above your head, then finally the stellar gateway, which is connected to your home planet. (You have now opened up your body, ready to receive the high vibrational healing).

INVOKE THE HEALING

Spirit team, I call upon you to imbue my energy field with the highest possible energy suitable for me. As I picture this golden elixir surging through my body, starting from my stellar gateway chakra, moving down through my body via the chakras, I know that it is flushing out all the energetic imprints from the effects of the vaccines. I also know that it is cleansing and purifying my body, and is returning my DNA to it's original intended status. Leaving my body, pure, perfect, and as God intended.

Repeat the Mantra x3

"I am pure, I am perfect, I am as God intended"
"I am pure, I am perfect, I am as God intended"
"I am pure, I am perfect, I am as God intended"   x3

Repeat the above mantra, as many times as you like, in sets of 3. As you are saying it out loud, imagine your body becoming brighter, lighter, purer. Letting go of anything in your body that does not serve your highest good.

CUT ANY CHORDS AND ATTACHMENTS

Call upon Archangel Michael to assist you cut any energetic chords or attachments accumulated due to the vaccines, that are not serving your highest good. Imagine holding a large pair of scissors, and imagine any chords and attachments being cut away. Knowing that you are fully free now of the effects of the vaccines.

STRENGTHEN YOUR CONNECTION TO THE GREAT SPIRIT

The stronger your connection to the Great Spirit, the more power you will have to determine your own health and well-being. Since everything is about frequency, and your intention is to raise your frequency above that of side effects and disease, the stronger your connection to spirit, the higher your frequency will be. If you do this protocol without fully committing your heart and soul, then the less effective it will be. If on the other hand you have seen the light, and are fully committed to walking the spiritual path, then this protocol is sure to work, as your frequency will match the intention.

GIVE THANKS, CLOSE THE SPACE

We thank all those who have taken part in this practice, including Archangel Michael, our own spirit team and helpers, and those that have specifically come in to help with this protocol.

Thank you, Thank you, Thank you.
It is done, It is done, It is done.

Spiritual Protection - In chapter 1 we have learned how to open up a sacred space, that will offer spiritual protection, by ensuring that we call upon only the beings with the highest and best intentions for all concerned. This is essential when undertaking any spiritual activity, I cannot express this enough. Like I mentioned, if you are relatively new to this work, if it seems complicated, then just simply remember to ask Archangel Michael to protect you, that will be enough. I am going to show you other ways of protecting yourself, including daily practices and regular practices, that will enhance your life, and be beneficial to our energy field.

It is good practice to call in Archangel Michael, and your spirit team when engaging in any spiritual practice, and especially when undertaking any clearing work. But ultimately your vibration is your greatest protector when it comes to spiritual protection. If your vibration is high enough, your frequency will zap anything of a low vibration that has a negative intent. On my home planet of Rycia (see my first book Enchanted Earth), since this is an enlightened planet, as a collective we use our vibration to protect our planet from any attacks from negative ET's. If we decode an imminent attack, everyone unites in actively raising their personal vibration, and becoming so high vibed, that nothing can penetrate the energy field of the planet. Love really does conquer all.

On the flip side to that, if you are in fear, then you are much more open to attack. Demons like nothing more than a fearful person, because a fearful person is easy to manipulate and control. Therefore, negative entities love to create fear, so they can more easily take away your power. You only have to observe how much the mainstream whipped up a constant state of fear and anxiety over the last few years, to see this in action, frighted a population into complying with tyranny. One of my roles on the astral planes is that of spiritual warrior, I regularly battle with demons. At this level it is a battle of wills, I am not scared or frightened of any of them, I stand steadfast in my power, and hold tight to my knowing. If I were to allow any sort of fear whatsoever into my energy field, it would be game over and they would win the battle. It is the same when I am doing my energy clearing work on the earth plane. If I were to get the slightest chink in my aura, then I would be become vulnerable, therefore, I make a point of maintaining a healthy aura for maximum protection.

The Aura - The aura is our own personal energetic space that surrounds our body. The aura is changeable, our mood, emotions, level of vibration and spiritual development will impact on the colour and essence of our aura. For example, someone who is full of love and good intent, and in a good place may have an aura that extends far out beyond their physical body, and it may contain beautiful pristine colours, such as pinks, blues, greens, purple. On the other hand, someone who is self-interested, angry and bitter may have a murky aura tight to their body, it might be muddy brown, grey or darkly coloured.

Contain your energy field/aura – When I am at home, or out in nature, my auric field extends out, I am open to the universal energy, and I am at one with my surroundings. When I go to busy places, such as supermarkets, shopping centres (malls), airports, I mindfully pull in my auric field, because I don't want to open to the chaotic energy of these places. I would do this by imagining my aura pulling in. Then I would surround myself in a protective auric bubble, and fill the bubble with light, that is vibrating at a 5D frequency or higher at all times. In this way, I can engage in my surroundings, but I don't allow my energy field to get contaminated by the chaotic energy, and by doing this, I am not allowing others to drain my energy, or my frequency to drop.

Often empaths report feeling exhausted when they are in crowds of people, this is because they fail to contain their energy field by creating a protective bubble before they leave their safe space, so therefore their energy field gets depleted and they feel wiped out and drained of their energy. It is a mistake to think that you get drained because you must be super-spiritual, or that you get exhausted following energy work, or giving reiki, simply because you did such a great job. If this is the case then you are getting drained because something is out of alignment, it's fantastic that you are doing the spiritual work, but you need to look after yourself, and your energy field, by exercising wise compassion, and mindfully taking care of your auric field. If you have a robust connection to source, then the energy work you do will actually energise you, not deplete you.

It is good daily spiritual hygiene to be mindful of your aura, and to take responsibility for your energy field, by protecting yourself using the above methods, by doing so, you are stepping further into your magical power, and creating the life you want, I keep repeating this message, but we really are the creators of our lives, if you don't want to feel depleted or ill, do something about it by protecting yourself. During the fake covid era, I regularly employed the force-field auric bubble strategy to avoid experiencing shedding from vaccinated people I imagined the force field around me, and knew that the shedding could not penetrate my energy field. I also do this around people who are sick, I put in the spiritual protection, and rise above the frequency of illness, as a result I usually enjoy very good health indeed. Remember, imagination is `everything, it is the creative force in 5D, so by imagining this, you are creating your reality.

CREATING A PYRAMID FORCE FIELD
MEDITATION GUIDE

Many of us take time and effort to keep our homes clean and tidy. We may regularly vacuum, dust and mop the floors, and probably get a sense of satisfaction when our homes are well presented. But how many of us regularly clear the energetic space in our homes? Perhaps we may burn incense, candles or sage regularly to help neutralise energy, but there is more we can do to help protect our homes energetically from the elements, from unwanted visitors from the 4th dimension, as well as negative ET's. It is possible to quite literally create an energetic force-field around our space, simply by setting our magical intention.......here's how:-

INVOCATION/PROTECTION

Take some deep breaths, put aside all the cares of the day. Take some more deep breaths, connect yourself, to yourself in this moment. Call in Archangel Michael, and your team of helpers. For me that would be the dragons, the unicorns, my ancestors the higher Galactic's, and Archangel Raphael, you may well have your own unique team, but always call in Archangel Michael, as he offers protection. For this meditation, we need to call in Archangel Gabriel, Archangel Zadkiel and Archangel Metatron, (as well as Archangel Michael and Archangel Raphael) as the angels are going to help us make the energy grid.

As I call these in, I am making it very clear, that I am only calling those in with the highest and best intention for all concerned. The highest and the best for everyone. We know now that we have the protection of the Archangels and all those mentioned, and they are coming in on the vibration to serve the highest and best for humanity and all concerned.

SET THE INTENTION

Great spirit, Divine light of Source, we give our heartfelt thanks, for everything we have received so far on our journeys. Today, Great Spirit, we ask that you may assist the angels, as we energetically grid this space, leaving a protective pyramid shaped force-field of 5th dimensional (or higher) energy.

COMMUNICATE DIRECTLY WITH THE ARCHANGELS

We would like to let you know that we love, honour and respect you, our dear friends from the angelic realms, and from our radiant golden hearts to yours we send our love and gratitude for all the help and assistance you have given humanity. We are asking you today, to help us create a pyramid of energy around this space (your home and garden, work space, whatever place you would like to grid), so that it can assist us to stay in 5D or higher vibration at all times.

SET UP THE GRID

We are going to set up a square around your space, you can do this in person, by walking around the perimeters of the space you wish to grid, or if it is not suitable to physically grid your place you can imagine it. If possible, use a crystal to place at each corner. Any crystal will do, or if you don't have any crystals to hand just use a stone, or a piece of wood, anything organic. Just make sure that you have programmed the crystal to be operating at 5D or higher. Once we have placed a crystal at each corner, we are then going to go to the middle of the square, and place another crystal in the middle, then we are going to imagine that middle point, rising in the air, and the four corners meeting the raised central point, to make a pyramid shape.

If you know which direction is north, then stand and face the north, if you are not sure which direction is north, it doesn't matter, imagine a north. As you face north, call in Archangel Michael. Archangel Michael is the protector, his blue cloak offers protection, and his sword is the sword of truth. Ask Archangel Michael to anchor his energy into this point.

Turn to face the south, and call in Archangel Gabriel. Archangel Gabriel is all about purity, he comes on a shimmering white vibration, purifying the earth and assisting the manifestation of 5D. Ask Archangel Gabriel to anchor his energy into this point.

Turn and face the west, call in Archangel Raphael, he is the healing angel, and emanates a beautiful green light, he also helps us step into abundance consciousness. Ask Archangel Raphael to anchor his energy into this point.

Turn and face the east, call in Archangel Zadkiel, Archangel Zadkiel oversees the violet ray of transmutation. He helps clean and purify energy. Ask Archangel Zadkiel to anchor his energy into this point.

Finally, move to the middle of the square, and call in Archangel Metatron. Archangel Metatron comes in on a vibrant orange and golden ray, he is overseeing the ascension process, and assists in the anchoring of the light. Ask Archangel Metatron to anchor his energy into this point.

From the central point, imagine pulling the energy up in the air, then all four corners link to the centre to make a pyramid shape. Now we ask that the Christ Light, and the Light of Mahatma is added to this pyramid of light, and ask that the space contained within the pyramid, remains at a frequency of 5D or higher at all times.

You have now made a pyramid shaped force-field of energy, that will protect your space. It is good practice to regularly reinforce the pyramid. Afterall, you would vacuum and mop your house regularly, so ideally you would re-energise your pyramid too. I do this by regularly thanking each Archangel in turn, and by mindfully topping up the light of Christ and Mahatma.

GIVE THANKS, CLOSE THE SPACE

We thank all those who have taken part in this practice, we give particular thanks to Archangel Michael, Archangel Gabriel, Archangel Raphael, Archangel Zadkiel and Archangel Metatron, as well as to our own team of guides, and the Great Spirit.

Thank you, Thank you, Thank you.
It is done, It is done, It is done.

Manifestation and Abundance Consciousness – Another way we can create the life we want is to hone in on our manifestation skills, and ensure we are living in abundance consciousness. Like attracts like, the universe will respond to whatever signals we put out there. It's like an energetic frequency match, if you are in a music shop, and you play a note on a guitar, all the other guitars will naturally vibrate and attune to the same note. In the same way, if you are in poverty consciousness, always feeling a lack, then the universe will respond, and it will feel like a constant struggle to make ends meet. The dark forces have plundered our resources, but worse of all, they have conditioned the minds of people to believe that life will always be a struggle, and that we don't deserve to be in abundance. It's that brainwashing and the perpetuation of the lack mentality that has kept the masses in chains for so long, meanwhile the elites have been eating cake, whilst throwing us the odd stale crumb here and there.

The new climate hoax agenda, is the latest attempt to keep us feeling guilty about having anything at all, they would love us to own nothing! So I would say, stop feeling guilty about having "stuff". Obviously it's good to consider the origins of the goods you consume, it is never ok to exploit others, be it people or nature in the quest for ownership, and it is wise to buy local, support local businesses as opposed to the cabal corporations. But we seriously need to stop worrying about our "carbon footprint", it's all a hoax.

I would add here that some people have the mistaken belief, that to be "spiritual" means you have to live in poverty. Again, that is 3D programming from the dark forces. Remember, the religions that promote this philosophy want the masses to live in poverty, whilst they live in luxury. (you only have to see the beautiful old Vicarage, or Rectory cottages and gardens in the UK, they certainly did not live in poverty, even though they were preaching the virtues of poverty consciousness to their congregations), let alone the tons of gold hoarded underneath the Vatican! The new age movement also have been targeted by the dark forces to have this mindset, and in this community it is seen as virtuous to own nothing and be happy..... But my message is, it doesn't have to be this way, we were never supposed to live in poverty, we have had the free resources from mother earth stolen from us, we have complied our way into a position where we are paying for water, electricity, food, when actually it is our divine right to live in abundance, and have this for free.

Free energy is available from the ether, Nicola Tesla knew this, our civilisation prior to the last great reset by the cabal ran on free energy. They've stolen the technology, to keep us dependant on taxable fossil fuel, and to make us feel guilty about it, and to stop us pro-creating. I know a couple who are so bought into the climate hoax, despite always wanting children, they have sadly now decided not to have a baby, because they feel it is the right thing to do for the planet! Unfortunately, people have allowed themselves to be coerced down a path that is so far removed from their connection to the Great Spirit, that they are listing to the media rather than listening to their own sense of right and wrong.

Divorced from their spiritual connection, they are easy prey for the propaganda machines. This is another reason why enhancing your spiritual connection is a huge protector against the dark forces. The more you develop your spirituality and raise your vibration, the better your discernment skills will become, and you will be far less likely to fall into the latest marketing ploy from the cabal, i.e "Covid 19 Pandemic", "Stay Safe", "Vaccines are Safe and Effective", "Stop Oil", "15 minute Cities", "I Stand for Ukraine", "Wear a Mask", "Card Payment Only" "Cash not Accepted", "Electric Cars", "Eat Bugs", "Lab grown Fake Meat", "Climate Emergency" "Choose your Gender", "Men have Periods too", "Chest Feeding not Breast Feeding", "Almost Naked Transvestites Teaching Kids in Schools about Gender and Diversity" "Schools Teaching 4 year olds to Masturbate and be Sexually Active". All this is the psychopathic satanic agenda, but if you are closed off from your spiritual selves, you are far more likely to succumb to this non-sense.

The cabal plan their agendas for hundreds of years beforehand, it is inter-generational, not just something recently hashed together in a board room somewhere, you have to hand it to them, they have done a pretty good job, millions of people have fallen for their agenda, many sadly paying their lives for it. (See excess death rate following the fake covid vaccine roll-out). But in this latest plan to reset the world, they have failed to factor in several things; firstly, karmically their time is up, the agreements made at the fall of golden Atlantis have now expired, they did so in December 2012, that is why the Myan calendar proposed then as being the end of the world, it was, the end of the old paradigm, but the cabal refused to hand in the keys. The second thing is that astrologically their time is up too, the age of Aquarius is upon us now, this era will be much fairer, and built on the divine feminine, and the divine masculine being in complete harmony, rather than the 3D masculinity that has dominated the world during the last age. They also failed to factor in the grand rising of consciousness, and the exponential amount of light being anchored into the planet currently, not to mention the amount of star seeds, like you and me, that have volunteered to incarnate during these unique times, to ensure the bringing in of the new Golden Age.

In April 2020, when much of the world was grasped by hysteria about a fake plandemic, I knew we were stepping into the time I had been preparing for my whole life, or even life-times.

Here is a poem I wrote in April 2020, just three weeks into the convid hoax.

2020 Vision

Wash your hands, now use gel
You must stand back in lockdown hell
Don't visit loved ones, stay at home
The "perfect citizen" lonely and alone

Cancelled, cancelled, cancelled
Your plans, your hopes your dreams
Is this the timely wake-up call, in fact
Life is not all it seems

Look beyond the outer surface
Who's really calling the shots?
Chasing carefully placed agenda's
We the unconscious robots....

Yet the inner voice gently
whispers in your ear,
Wake up my friend
It's time to see things clear

Rich celebrities, so valued for their fake nails and fake tan
During lockdown what are they doing to help fellow man?
It's the minimum wage warriors, that are keeping us alive
Toiling on as usual, working hard just to survive

Lets evaluate our systems
Together we've the power to change
Revolution of the mind-set
That keeps us all in chains

You have your inner-wisdom
21st century living has buried deep within
But lock-down is the perfect time
To open up and let it in

Greedy corporations exploiting workers
Wanting more and more
Lets buy from local businesses
A local economy like times before

Think about your purchases
Do you really need that sweat-shop produced dress
Do you need that plastic item
Who are you trying to impress?

Wash your hands, now use gel
You must stand back in lockdown hell
Don't visit loved ones, stay at home
The "perfect citizen" lonely and alone

During a meditation, my guides showed me a very clear vision. I saw some architectural drawings of a bridge. The plans were very meticulous and detailed, these plans were symbolic of the cabal's plan to take total control of the world, and do another reset. This time, merging artificial intelligence with humans, to develop almost soulless transhuman robotic slaves, that were at the total mercy of their controllers. However, I saw that the bridge did not meet in the middle, and the drawings were in the preliminary colour, of faded grey, not solid. My guides very clearly told me that the bridge would never cross, and the grey faded drawings were also symbolic that it was just a plan not a reality. The vision was extremely clear and vivid, I received the message from spirit loud and clear.

From then onwards, I was able to step into this era with confidence, whilst everyone else was falling into fear and concern, I knew there was absolutely nothing at all to fear. Having said this, I also knew that we create our own reality, just because I had seen this vision, didn't mean I was going to avoid taking responsibility, disengage, and do nothing. I attended many freedom rallies all over the England clearly stating I do not consent to their mandates. I also made a point of sharing my knowledge, to help to stem the fear. Spirit also encouraged me to start a Youtube channel, and offer my spiritual services (gillianengland.com) to further help the masses during those times. People have said to me countless times, that they wished they had my confidence to know that all would be well. Lets look at this for a moment, the reason I have so much confidence that all is well, is because I have a strong connection to the Great Spirit. I was able to receive a direct message, and see for myself, no middle man necessary, just myself and my guides. Is that not even more incentive to develop your spiritual awareness and improve your connection to the Great Spirt?

CHAPTER 6
DEEP DIVE INTO OTHER REALMS

If you are familiar with my work, or have read my first book "Enchanted Earth", you will know that I talk quite freely about my off-world heritage, and my home planet of Rycia, which is located in a different galaxy, trillions of miles away. Many of you reading this will also have star-seed energy. When you first consider this, it can seem quite daunting, a little scary, or at least a bit "woo woo". But as we step into 5D existence, and engage with our multi-dimensional selves, this phenomenon will seem natural and normal, part of everyday life, after all, in bygone cycles of life on earth, receiving benign star races on our planet was not in the least bit uncommon, and accepted as normal.

It is only since the invasion of the reptilian races, (who's controllers are ultimately AI) that our interactions with off-world visitors have taken a nefarious turn (There are very small percentage of reptilians that are good, but by enlarge, most reptilian ET's are nefarious). Percentage wise, most of our off-world visitors are benign and helpful to us. Some are neutral, and neither wish us good or bad, but some are evil and want to use our resources for their own ends. This includes our minerals, metals including gold, silver and platinum, but worse of all, some ET races, including the reptilians eat humans just like we eat chicken and beef! They especially like eating infants, with a certain blood type, and of course there is the organ harvesting, child trafficking, satanic rituals and terrorising children so that they secrete potent adrenaline, which they harvest and produce the adrenochrome.

The reptilians have infiltrated our communities by pretending to be humans, they can shape-shift and take the form of a human, then breed with organic humans to produce reptilian hybrids. (high chance the psychopaths and narcissists are the reptilians or the hybrids). The reptilian races that shape-shift into humans, have to apply some effort in order to remain in a human appearance, otherwise they will morph back into their reptilian selves. If they get sexually aroused, they often will shape shift back into the reptile state. This is why those taking part in satanic rituals wear robes, not everyday clothing. If they are wearing robes, when they change back to a reptile, they won't rip the clothing. Another thing that helps them to keep in the human form, is to take adrenochrome, by regularly drinking the substance produced from the blood of terrorised children, they can manage the shape shifting better. Sadly their sick need for adrenochrome has been the driving force behind the horrendous child trafficking industry, that has been going on for hundreds if not thousands of years. Many of the truth warriors working so fastidiously against this terrible industry, are most likely re-incarnated victims of such activities, they have most probably experienced this first hand in past lives, and have resolved to come back and help get rid of it.

We know that the TV and movie industry have produced films that show us what the dark forces are up to. In this way, they believe they have sought our consent. In their warped twisted minds, they think that if they have showed us, then we have consented (another example of them taking implied consent if we don't specifically state we do not consent). The signalling in movies is rife, think of the incredible hulk, he gets angry and rips his cloths (signalling reptilians shape-shifting out of their clothing), think of Monster's Inc. they terrorise children in order to harvest energy (signalling to adrenochrome production). The Disney films are the worst, there is satanic signalling in every movie. Did you know that convicted child trafficker Ghislane Maxwell used to work for Disney, as a show compare in the 1980's? Personally, I've always had a very strong aversion to the whole Disney brand, energetically I couldn't stand it, and I have turned down several opportunities to visit their parks, but it is only recently that I've realised why. Always trust your gut instinct, it will never let you down.

DUMBS – Deep Underground Military Basis – If you have only recently experienced your spiritual awakening, and are new to these sort of concepts, this can all seem a bit far-fetched, and you might be asking questions as to how on earth all of this could be co-ordinated? Well I am sorry to say, that it has been co-ordinated very efficiently, in deep underground military basis across the entire planet. Yes, almost all of the world governments have been involved, un-beknown to the average voting citizen.

I am no military expert, so for extensive details seek research from other sources, but my understanding is that initially the US government did a deal with nefarious ET races, agreeing to trade in human beings (for meat, adrenochrome, and breeding experiments) and other earth resources (metals, minerals), in exchange for off-world advanced technology. As the world powers merged, the networks spread around the world. This is another incentive for the one world governments, they wanted to be able to control the entire world, and any nation not complying has been targeted by the US military.

The DUMBS consist of a network of subterranean tunnels linking cities across the entire planet. They have used advanced technology to create these places, and the use electromagnetic energy for the transport systems in the tunnels. You could get to Australia from the UK in a matter of minutes. The scale of these underground cities and networks is absolutely immense, like I said, the entire globe has been contaminated, with certain areas being particular hot spots.

As well as using these deep underground basis for child trafficking, adrenochrome production and human trafficking, they have been a hub for genetic experiments. Gross as it sounds, they had huge laboratories, where they merged human DNA with other ET races, and animals, to create hideous hybrid creatures, the stuff of night mares. Another upsetting fact is that they have kept child-bearing aged women captive, often in cages, simply as "breeders", forcing them to produce children, that they can use for meat, satanic rituals and adrenochrome production.

I know that reading about this can be very disturbing, but the average person at least needs to acknowledge this has been going on. Like I said earlier, to deny this stuff is protecting the perpetrators. You don't have to seek out the disturbing images of this kind of thing, but we owe it to the victims, to at least acknowledge that it has been happening. We need to see and honour these souls, so that energetically they can be set free. Better still, lets set a collective effort of sending each and every soul that has been abused in this way, our love, light and healing. Lets ask for an angel to accompany every one of them, and do the Restore, Refresh Re-energise meditation to clear the energy.

Earlier in the book, I mentioned the concept of 4th dimensional creatures on the astral planes. In the DUMBS we can find physical manifestations of these monsters, they can manifest here due to the fact the vibration of the space is so low. It really isn't pretty. I love nature, and most bugs and creepy crawlies don't bother me in the slightest. However, I have a very strong aversion to large black spiders, the ones with prominent black bodies and legs, I don't mind the lighter coloured garden spiders at all. During my energetic clearing work of the DUMBS I have come across the chimera spiders. These are a race of huge black spiders, with very nefarious intentions, that have taken residence in the DUMBS. If you have read Tolkien's Lord of the Rings, his reference to the Shelob gives a flavour of these creatures. They are simply evil, and are often used to terrorise the children in order to produce adrenochrome. My higher dimensional self has had many a battle with these demons, and I realise now that my arachnophobia is based on past-life experiences. Interestingly when I visited Ireland, there was a distinct theme of chimera spiders across many sites I cleared, same as on Holy island, in Northumberland, UK, there was a satanic obelisk where a huge chimera spider had taken residence, my dragons and I soon transmuted it's energy lets just say!

Most of my knowledge of the DUMBS has come from my own experiences of working to clear them. I do this remotely, and can see what's going on in a remote viewing type of way. It came to my attention that there have been huge laboratories, where communities of nefarious ET's have been storing human DNA. My understanding is that they began by harvesting the DNA of the Chinese population. I cannot describe how many samples they had, thousands upon thousands. Using their technology, they desperately wanted to be able to create their own human from scratch. They have been experimenting with cloning and replicating humans, but the fact of the matter is, in order to create even a clone, they need some original DNA of an organic human. The God spark prevails, but they are conceited enough to believe they can create without it.

Following on from the Chinese, they then targeted other races. Many people fell for the hoax of things such as "Ancestor Today, send us your DNA and we will tell you if you are related to Queen Victoria or Robin Hood!". This was little more than a trick to get you to consent to giving away your precious DNA. Then we move on to the fake convid PCR test, what do you think the real reason for that was? Yes you've got it, for the dark forces to harvest even more DNA, from consenting humans! You've got to understand that this was a huge co-ordinated project with the world governments all colluding. On the one hand they were creating fear about a fake disease, (great for collecting loosh), secondly they were normalising the restriction of movement in preparation for the climate hoax 15 minute city agenda, (stay home, stay safe), thirdly they were collecting DNA (PCR test), whipping up so much fear about a fake disease, that people would feel relieved when offered a deadly, untested fake vaccine (which was really a DNA altering drug), can't you see how desperate they are to interfere and change our precious and unique DNA?

I smelled a rat about this from the start, and was telling everyone that the PCR test was little more than a scam to get you to part with your DNA profile. I have not done a single PCR test, and never will, I am willing to forego anything that necessitates doing one, I made this very clear from the start, that is where I draw my own personal line. I was determined about this because I know that our DNA is our unique signature, no one in the universe has the same DNA as you! This is such a precious resource, one we are yet to fully understand, but as with the Disney situation, I am following my instinct on this, and I know it will not let me down. Again, the reason I was able to see this clearly before most others could see it, was simply because of my strong connection to the Great Spirit. Yet another example of how a strong connection to our spiritual selves is a great protective factor.

Clearing the DUMBS – I have no doubts at all that there has been a huge co-ordinated effort from the good forces, white hats, good military, call them what you will to clear up the DUMBS world-wide. From a remote viewing perspective, I have seen this with my own eyes, or should I say third eye. I have been doing clearing work for many years, but the DUMBS clearing work for me, consciously started in 2020. Other healers and energy workers may have their own methods, but for me I first of all put my protection in place, set my intention to help, then tune into the space I am assisting with. Often I will open up my personal energy portal, opening up my 12 chakras. I have noticed that when I am doing live work, i.e there are living incarnated souls involved, Commander Ashtar often appears. His ship or should I say, a ship will be hovering above the site I am clearing. I then allow Commander Ashtar and team to step into the space and enter the earth plane and this space, using my physical body, i.e the portal I have created via my chakra systems, they enter the space and do the work, a bit like a team of paratroopers ascending from a helicopter onto a battle ground, Commander Ashtar and team ascend from their ships in the sky down via my body portal, to the DUMBS. This works because of my free will as an organic human being on this earth plane, and also because of my high vibrational state.

From this point onwards, I just let them get on with it, I don't need to get involved seeing what's going on, unless I chose to. I have seen them rescuing child-bearing women and children kept like animals in cages, I have seen the results of beings made from cloning, and genetic experiments. Now I know what's been going on, and now I can honour the souls of these people, I don't need to keep visiting it. Like I say, I offer them my body as a vessel in that moment, and add my energy to it, but I don't need to keep seeing the gory details. Time is an illusion, so I give them the permission to keep this going for as long as necessary, meanwhile, I can go back to my daily life, knowing that they will use the energy of my intention for as long as they need to. Before

I depart from this, I always send my dragons there to transmute the energy, I see my dragons breathing their fire of transmutation into that space. I finish off by doing the Restore, Refresh, Re-energise and imagining the golden elixir energy coming down from the universe the seven suns and my home planet, coursing through my body, into the DUMBS. This is like pouring extremely high-vibe energy into the space, this will change up the entire vibration of the space, and therefore will help and assist any of the rescuing endeavours that are taking place.

You might be thinking how on earth can that be possible, how can that possibly work because I am not physically there in the DUMBS. But remember, in the 5th dimension, energy and matter take on very different properties, intention and frequency are everything. If you try to understand energy work from a 3D perspective, of course this will seem impossible, but viewed from a 5D multi-dimensional place, this makes complete sense.

This energetic clearing of the DUMBS has worked hand in hand with the boots on the ground third dimensional good military. What you also have to remember, is that the 3D good military have access to advanced technologies, that viewed from an everyday lay person perspective may also seem impossible. Take for example the rescued children, what happens to them, where do they go? It is my understanding that they are taken to healing sanctuaries, to receive intense physical and psychological healing. This is on a different dimension, either off planet, or to hidden parts of planet earth, such as Antarctica where there are advanced technologies and methods (med beds, energy healing), where they can receive all the help they need. I believe that the transportation systems used to carry the children from these situations would supersede any technology that is currently out in the public domain.

I am now going to share another insight, regarding the children in the DUMBS. I saw this in 2020, and it has helped me to deal with the horrors of what has been going on. I mentioned above about the extensive breeding and genetic experiments that have been taking place in the DUMBS. When I had a closer look at this (remotely), I could see that they use the DNA from a sample (human), then use a fractal of this DNA to produce and replicate clones, of said sample human. Lets imagine then that they had taken a sample of my DNA, and had made 20 clones of Gillian. When the good military rescued the children, unfortunately many of them died, they just couldn't make it. This was naturally very upsetting, but what spirit told me, was that it would be the 20 clone Gillian's that died so to speak, and that the original Gillian would most likely survive, because it would be the original Gillian that had the God spark, the breath of life, had the Great Spirit contained within. This helped me immensely to deal with all that I saw. Cloning is an abomination of God, so when the clones do not survive, it is fitting with the universal laws that they don't. When we comprehend this, it is easier to bear, and is another example of where we need to raise above our emotional state, and see the bigger picture, and is further evidence of how when we have a strong connection to the Great Spirit, it makes things such as this much easier to deal with. Wise compassion again.

DON'T CONFUSE THE 5D INNER-EARTH BEINGS
WITH THE DUMBS

Some of you may be familiar with the concept of Telos/Agartha and the Inner Earth/ Hollow Earth, this civilisation is something completely different from the nefarious tunnel systems and DUMBS, and not to be confused with it. The Hollow Earth/ Inner Earth civilisation is another subterranean world, underground, an advanced civilisation operating on the 5th dimension or higher. These ancient human beings retreated to the Hallow Earth, when the reptilian races started to assert their regressive agendas and plunder the surface of earth. The Inner Earth beings have been allowed to evolve unhindered, without the constant re-sets perpetuated by the negative ET's, also there has been no child trafficking or adrenochrome production, and life has been good for everyone. As a result they have evolved as was intended for all earth dwellers, they live in total alignment with the natural laws of the planet. They are completely stepped into their power of creator beings, able to create the weather systems they want, to manifest anything they see fit, have access to free nourishing food, pristine water, energy and transportation systems. They also only work for a maximum of four hours per day, the rest of the time is spent in leisure, spiritual development and socialising. They live in complete harmony with each other, as well as with the natural world. The landscape is just like we have here on the surface, mountains, oceans, lakes, although everything is on a much larger scale. If you have ever seen photo's of the giants of Tartaria, then these are more than likely Inner Earth beings, since they have been able to live pristine lives, their life spans can last hundreds if not thousands of years, as they are attuned to regeneration and creation, so they often choose to live very long lives.

Whilst doing my energy work, I have come across several portals to the Inner Earth, and have communicated with Inner Earth beings. They are our human brothers and sisters that look just like you and me, only at the very least seven feet tall! They tell me that they have had to close down the portals, to keep their world pure, and stop contamination from the surface world. They have told me that when the time is right, when the 5th dimensional shift has taken place, then they will open up the portals, and come to assist us build our new earth. They will share with us the technology, and teach us methods of manifestation and transportation, as well as share their spiritual insights. This will not be interfering with the natural evolution of earth at all, as they are truly our Earth brothers and sisters, we too could have evolved in this way on the surface, if we had not been repeatedly plundered, regressed and repressed by the negative ET's that had taken control of the surface of our beautiful planet. I am personally really looking forward to the time when the Inner Earth beings make an appearance, in fact I have offered to be an ambassador for them, and act as an intermediary between them and our regular humans.

OFF-WORLD CONNECTIONS

When I was a child, I used to stare up to the sky and marvel at the stars, I had a feeling and indeed a knowing that there were other civilisations out there. I used to play games with my friends in the school playground, where we would imagine we were aliens, twirl around and hold pretend conversations with our mother planets. When I look back at this now, I realise that what may have been seen as silly childish game, were actually my attempts to consciously integrate and acknowledge my ET heritage.

It's only in the last ten years or so, that I've been able to consciously attune to my home planet, and gain further clarity. I'd visited my home planet in meditations, and whilst opening myself to psychic art, had sketched images of the beings that reside on my home planet. However, it was not until I sat down to channel information for my first book, Enchanted Earth, that I really stepped into the details of my star heritage. Even for me, I was a bit surprised at what came out with this channelling. Even though I considered myself awake, and unprogrammed, I still had to let go of some conditioning I had picked up along the way, and truly open my heart and mind, in order to receive the information. If you are currently on this journey, opening up to your own star heritage, I would suggest that you be as open minded as possible, and don't try to fit the information to a narrative you feel is acceptable. It really is about just letting go and trusting, and remember, you won't be able to fit 5D or higher concepts into a 3D world!

I believe that most of you reading this will be star seeds, from different planets, that have specifically volunteered to incarnate on earth at this time, to assist with the earth's ascension. The fact that you are open to reading a book such as this, means that you can see further along the road than the average citizen, and are most likely stepped into your spiritual selves, which will ultimately lead you to questioning your true heritage. We have been programmed to believe that we are the only planet with sentient inhabitation in the universe. There are a few reasons why they (the former controllers of the world) wanted us to believe this. They wanted us to live with blinkers on, believing, unquestionably in the perpetual lies and propaganda they spewed out, because if we knew of our star heritage, and knew how powerful each and every one of us are as creator beings, then government policies, government mandates and politicians start to look irrelevant, we realise there is a far bigger picture playing out, and we would see that we are more than capable of governing ourselves, based on universal laws and principles, instead of government policies.

We realise we don't need laws and rules put in place by the dark forces to keep us enslaved, whilst keeping them in positions of power. It's literally game over for the globalists. As more and more people have been waking up to this, they know they are losing power. Hence the clown-like ridiculous politics of the last few years. They are panicking, they know their time is up, so are throwing everything they can think of at us, in an attempt to keep control. They are wasting their time, God wins.

Remember, since the earliest days of sentient habitation on planet earth, we have naturally had interaction with our galactic brothers and sisters from other planets, and different dimensions. In earlier phases of life on earth, this was seen as natural, and would be a normal everyday occurrence. However since the fall of golden Atlantis, we have been placed in a type of inter-planetary quarantine, whereby for the average citizen galactic travel has not been an option. The fact that we have been operating on the 3rd dimension has been a huge factor in this, but also it has been for protection as much as anything else, a form of damage limitation, since the dark forces were holding the power, a quarantine was necessary. Now the dark forces have lost their grip of control, and as we step back into the 5th dimension and our multi-dimensional selves, we will naturally become attuned to our star planets and intergalactic travel will be open to the average citizen.

In my visions, I've seen myself traversing space, travelling from my home planet of Rycia, to and from planet earth. When I first started seeing myself doing this, I thought that it was just my consciousness travelling, and that my physical avatar did not go anywhere. I had clear visions or "dreams" of me travelling through space, and seeing landscapes of other planets. Some that had aspects similar to planet earth, others that bore no resemblance at all.

I've looked into this further, and it is my understanding that, yes on one hand my consciousness travels the said distances, but also my organic DNA somehow merges with an off-world type of plasma substance, and forms a kind of space craft. My consciousness and DNA operate and navigate the space craft. It's like it is a living organism. Earlier in the book I mentioned the uniqueness of our DNA, and how precious it is. It is my understanding that it is the codes within my DNA that enable me to access and create my space craft, no wonder the dark forces have been harvesting millions of samples of DNA, and have been trying to replicate the God spark! I appreciate that as a human being living in 3D, that has been programmed, this is difficult to conceptualise. But like I mentioned earlier, one thing I have come to learn, whilst opening up my conscious mind to my off-world heritage, is to not try to squash off-world stuff into human concepts!

Interacting with ET's - If you mention the word Alien, or UFO, most people would instantly get a feeling of fear in their bodies. This is because of the conditioning propagated by Hollywood, and US military. They wanted us to be fearful of any ET's, because the last thing they wanted was for us to be open to our true, fantastic, powerful star heritage. Having said that, make no mistake, there have been very nefarious ET's working alongside the US military (and other world militaries) that have been trafficking humans, organ harvesting, abducting them for genetic experiments and the like, so for our own sakes, it is wise to be cautious. Although for the most part the nefarious activities of the Greys have now been shut down, and despite the fact that most ET's here now are benign and wish us no harm, it is important to remember that there is always a chance of nefarious ET's entering our planet, using cloaking technology, that distorts and hides their frequency. So it is important to use your discernment, and there are a few golden rules I suggest you apply when interacting with any ET's;

• Firstly, always clearly state that you do not consent to being abducted. (Remember what I said about implied consent, if you don't explicitly state you do not consent, then nefarious ones will take that as consenting).

• Ask them to identify themselves. Universal law says that they must truly identify themselves. If they give you false information then they are contravening that law, and will have to face the consequences.

• Remember to ask for your spiritual protection, Archangel Michael and your own team of spirit guides.

• Tell them you are of the highest light, and clearly state "I am the love, I am the light, I embody the Christ light". (if they are bad and are trying to deceive you they will not be able to stand this vibration, and it might be enough to make them disappear)

• Consciously emanate light from your very being (again this will help you to discern their true intention, as the good ones will thrive on the light, but the bad ones will disappear, or you will be able to see their true colours).

• Ask them for the reason for the interaction. Speak with them, there won't be any language barriers, you will be communicating on a consciousness vibration, where all languages are understood.

• If you want to invoke communication with ET's be careful who you call up. It's a good idea to ask to connect with your own star family, not just randomly call up anyone. After putting in your protection, you could say something on the lines of "I am open to seeing my star brothers and sisters, and my own galactic family, I am making it clear that I am only asking for interaction with those who have the highest and best intentions for all concerned".

Over the years, I have sat for many channelling sessions. I have invited in those from the higher realms, that have the highest and best intentions for those concerned. As a result of my invocation, I have welcomed a vast variety of ET beings to energetically join in the sacred space. I have not seen these physically, but have seen them in my minds eye. I have a main communications guide, called Red Feather, he acts as gate-keeper and master of ceremonies. As well as my own clairvoyant images, Red Feather has described many ET beings to me, and told me that they were very grateful to be invited to our circle as it gave them a very rare opportunity to observe our human way of life. Red feather also told me that many of them looked nothing like a human, many taking on huge statures. I know that on my home planet, Rycia, the native species are huge, golden bird-like creatures, not at all humanoid.

If I asked the average person to describe to me an alien, most people would describe the grey variety, with large black eyes. That's because that's the image Hollywood has projected, and I believe that was for a calculated reason, we now know the dark nature of Hollywood, and we also know that most of the Greys do not have humanity's best interests at heart. They have been working on behalf of the reptilians, and are programmed clones/minions doing the leg work (abductions, genetic experiments, organ harvesting, child trafficking) for the reptilians. By projecting Greys as the generic image of ET's, then in their warped way of thinking, they believe they are gaining consent. Also if people spend time focussing and thinking of the Greys, it energises them, and gives them energy. With that in mind, especially if you are open to seeing/communicating with UFO's or your star heritage, find another image to focus on, rather than the Greys, and remember the golden rules mentioned above.

CHAPTER 7

ENERGY WORK, SACRED SITE AND LEY LINES

As mentioned previously, my primary role in this lifetime is energy director. In a vision, I saw myself deciding my life-plan for this life. I saw myself sat on a sort of platform, looking out to the stars. My companion in this vision was Archangel Raphael, he helped me to plan this life, and has been helping me ever since. I clearly saw that my main work was to be around directing energy, this was also one of my roles on my home planet Rycia, where I would be tasked with sending energy to specific places in the universe. In this life, as Gillian England, I use this innate knowledge of energy to clear blocked ley lines, to energise specific energy points, to transmute lower vibrational entities, and I've also done extensive work to repair and revitalise the golden energy grid of the entire planet.

I am helped by my dragon team, I have a red dragon that is part of my higher-self, oversoul, and a green dragon that comes in on the vibration of Archangel Raphael. They are very powerful, benign beings, from the 13th dimension, that bring in much love and wisdom. I have very clear soul memories of having been incarnated as a red dragon (see my first book, Enchanted Earth), in the very earliest times of life on earth. At a time before time, when the earth was pristine and new, one of my tasks then was to help set up and create the energetic grid of the planet, ready for the in-coming inhabitants.

Interestingly in many cultures, ley lines are referred to as dragon lines, this fits with the ley line work I do, as the dragons are always there to help. In 2021, the dragons and I undertook some intensive work repairing the golden energy grid that covers planet earth. When I tuned in psychically, I could clearly see that there were parts of the grid that had been destroyed by the dark forces, and other parts that had been badly damaged, so we directed a lot of energy there to restore, refresh and re-energise these places. I intuitively knew what to do to repair them, as a part of my over-soul helped to create them in the first place! When the planetary energy grid is in good shape, it sets the framework for the rest of the planet, and the energies will flow as was intended by the Great Spirit.

In the English culture, dragons have been demonised. If you did an internet search for pictures of dragons, they are mostly depicted as dark and evil looking things. Or in mythology, there are tales of "slaying the dragon" and the story of George and the dragon, where the hero kills the dragon. This is another attempt by the dark forces of inverting the truth. The dark forces fear the light, so in their case they have got something to fear, that's perhaps why they have given them this unfair image. Just like the words Pagan, Gypsy or Weird, in mainstream they are often used in derogatory ways, yet to me they are referring to three cultures that hold wisdom of the Great Spirit, and esoteric knowledge.

Ley Lines - People often ask me what is a ley line? There are far more in-depth technical explanations available from other sources, however, my simple explanation is this:- The entire planet is covered in an energetic grid like magnetic system, the lines that form the grids are called ley lines. Think of it like this, no doubt you are aware that inside your body you have veins, arteries, and capillaries that carry the life-blood, oxygen and nutrients around your body, they are the transportation system within your body. Ley lines are like this, there are major ones (such as veins and arteries), then there will be smaller ones (such as capillaries).

The entire planet is covered in this grid system, although the UK and Ireland seem to have disproportionally high levels of ley lines, compared to the land mass of many other countries. I believe this is because the British Isles, and Ireland are ancient lands. They hold the keys and codes within the bedrock of the earth that are the remnants of previous ancient civilisations, including Atlantis and Egypt, but also civilisations that pre-date these. A recent visit to the Giant's Causeway in Ireland was evidence of this for me, I could clearly see remnants of ancient civilisations, such as giant petrified dragons and gigantic petrified tree stumps, but to the average 3D conditioned person, these would simply look like rocks and mountains.

Curiously, for such a relatively small landmass, most countries around the world have heard of the UK. Also the English language is widely spoken and is the most common second language in the world, which makes no sense at all, given how small the British Isles are, and the relatively small population. Some people think it is to do with the former British Empire, perhaps so, but my question would be, why did the former controllers of the planet choose the UK for the head quarters of their "empire"? It's to do with the energy they can harvest and use from the ley lines. Make no mistake, the dark forces have known all about the power of ley lines, and have been using them, themselves to enhance their powers. However, they have not wanted the masses to have any awareness of them, so that they could keep the masses is ignorance, and stop them stepping into their power. They purposely put out false information, market them to be ancient relics of an uncivilised, primitive past, and then purposely, block or harvested the energy for themselves.

Unblocking Ley Lines - On the video I did with fellow spiritual warrior, Mark Attwood, Adventures in a Cosmic Suite, "Unblocking the 5D sun in the Peak District" (see Mark Attwood's rumble channel) whilst at Arbor Low stone circle, a very important site in Derbyshire, UK, on the convergence of nine important ley lines, we discovered that nine concrete blocks had been deliberately placed on each of the ley lines, eight of the blocks had the inscription VR carved on them, which stands for Victoria Regina (Queen Victoria), and the ninth had the inscription GR which stands for George Regina (King George VI). During the filming, we discovered that the royal family had been harvesting the energy from these important ley lines, and no doubt had been using it for nefarious reasons.

We unblocked all of the ley lines, reclaimed the power and returned them to the light, just as we had finished unblocking the last line, the universe rewarded us with the most unbelievable, spectacular display of 5D sun plasma energy. It was a show like nothing I had ever seen before, it was absolutely amazing, the camera captured some of it, but not the entire spectrum. It was so exceptional, I will remember that 5D sun phenomena for the rest of my life, I also knew that the sun was emitting light keys and codes, to help upgrade our DNA, and enhance our spiritual gifts. I have experienced other weather phenomena after undertaking energy work at sacred sites, such as a storm coming out of nowhere, after clearing a concrete "map" at the top of Glastonbury Torr in England, and then a bolt of lightening struck right in front of my vehicle after re-energising Grianan of Aileach, a sacred site in Ireland, but nothing as off-the-charts spectacular as the Arbor Low experience.

Following on from that experience at Arbor Low, I made a point of purposely looking for other energy blockers, at other stone circles and sacred sites. Once you know what you are looking for, you'd be surprised at how many concrete structures have been deliberately placed to block ley lines. At another stone circle, near Eyam in Derbyshire, UK we found blocks with the letters FD inscribed on them, which stand for Fidei Defensor, a Latin word which means Defender of the Faith. Henry VIII was the first Defender of the

Faith, and it has been a title passed down through the royal family ever since. Again, I unblocked the energy, reclaimed it for the light, and did the restore, refresh, re-energise (RRR).

Next time you are out and about at your local sacred sites, keep an eye out for these energy blockers, often concreate blockers, disguised as maps, Trig points or information posts. Why not take your dowsing rods, and see for yourself, then you can do the RRR protocol (free at www.gillianengland.com), to help the cause...together we are stronger, we are brighter we are lighter......

I believe that ley lines are the transportation systems that carry electomagnetic energy around the planet. Although many of them are termed "tombs", from undertaking my own energy work I have found no evidence of them being tombs at all. I can clearly determine that many of the ancient sites, such as stone circles, cairns and pyramids are built on important energy centres or portals to other dimensions and believe that the ancient stone structures themselves were technology that was instrumental in capturing, and condensing the magnetic energy, then propelling the energy around the entire planet. Ancient advanced technology relied on electro-magnetic energy, and it is my understanding, that as we move back to 5D, we will have access to this once more. Remember, we had much more advanced technology in previous cycles of earth's existence, it is only since the negative, regressive ET's have taken control, that these electro magnetic systems have been hidden, and kept from the masses, as another way of controlling us.

The extensive energy work I have undertaken over the last ten years or so, has been to prepare the planet for the return of this electro magnetic energy. I have been visiting countless sacred sites, unblocking, restoring, refreshing and re-energising the sites, in Europe and the UK and the corresponding ley lines.

When I first started specifically visiting sites to clear them, I was visited by ascended master Merlin, he said he had come to help me with my work. There and then I made a deal, that if he arranged for the universe to provide me with the means to travel to the sites that needed assistance, then I would be of service. So far we have both kept to the bargain, (on the surface it may look as though I take a lot of holidays) but I simply marvel at how the universe conspires to get me to the places that need clearing. This includes random invitations to places, or finding myself somewhere that was totally unplanned, as well as changes to already made plans with circumstances beyond my control such as delays, cancelled flights, diversions roads closures, weather events etc.

It has given me a great lesson in trusting in the wisdom of the universe. Instead of worrying when things don't go to plan, when I'm faced with unexpected circumstances I just look out for the message from the divine. When I step into the rhythm of this work, I am truly living my best life, as I am in alignment with my soul purpose.

Tartaria and Nicola Tesla Energy - Many of you will be aware of the concept of Nicola Tesla's free energy. The idea of bringing in free energy from the ether. It is my belief, that in the non to distant future we will have access to this once again, that it will use the ley lines to transport it. Once you have been down the Tartaria rabbit hole, in Europe at least, you can see evidence of Tartaria structures in every town and city. During recent times, more than anything else, Tartaria was the one concept that I had to wake up to. I was already in touch with my spirituality, I already knew about satanic podophiles, and that all the world governments were run by shape-shifting reptilians, but I was not aware that in relevantly recent history we'd had magnificent buildings deliberately destroyed by the cabal, in order to irradicate the knowledge, as well as the structures that harnessed, stored and distributed free energy. Another consequence of them purposely destroying buildings was to bring the vibration down. Buildings and forms carry vibrational codes, the Tartarian buildings held beauty and a high vibe. The act of ripping them down, and replacing them with hideous concrete eyesores (concrete is a tremendous energy blocker), has brought the vibration down of such places. Of course, we are learning now that this has all been by design, in an attempt to lower our vibration, and keep us under their control.

In respect of Tartaria and the former free energy, once I'd discovered this, I had to go through a type of grieving process, grieving for the grace and beauty of this relatively recent lost civilisation, and the subsequent consequences on the human race.

Like mentioned previously, I am certain that ley lines play a key part in the distribution of this free electro magnetic energy, and I am looking forward to the time when we will no longer have to put up with the harmful EMF of electrical cables, running through our land and our homes, instead we will be using God's original, organic WIFI, the ether.

I'm also convinced that the recent unprecedented increase in energy prices, is to make us feel a pinch in our wallets and pay attention, so when it's time to reveal the truth about our stolen free energy technology, we will really see what the bad guys had intended for us, and it will have more of an affect since the energy bills have put so many people in poverty.

CHAPTER 8
FINAL THOUGHTS

Grieving Process - No matter where you are on your road to enlightenment, I am almost certain that from 2020 onwards, your life took on many significant and fundamental changes. Everybody in this community has had to deal with multiple losses. I mentioned that I went through a grieving process when I discovered Tartaria and the lost free energy, not to mention the multiple relationships, family, friends and community groups that have also fallen by the wayside, as my frequency has grown, and I am no longer compatible with their energy field.

I have no doubts at all, that as a collective we have all been through a mighty collective grieving process, and each of us will have our unique experience of this, because we each hold a unique life-view, or in other words, we each have our own blend of values and experiences, and attach different meanings to things. We have had to let go of so much over the last few years, many of you reading this will have lost marriages, jobs, friendships, hobbies and experienced fundamental changes, that have challenged the very bedrock of your sense of self.

To make it to this point, shows you are the strongest of the strong, and I salute you, I salute your authenticity, your courage, and your ability to listen to your higher self, no matter what others were saying about you, you had the courage to make it here, well done!

Not only have we experienced personal and relationship losses, our view on the lives we lead previously will never look the same again. For example, we no longer have the same interest in sport because we know it's rigged and that sporting events were used to cover up child trafficking. We no longer look up to Hollywood, TV and celebrity cultures, because we know that to be allowed to reach a level of success almost all have compromised their personal ethics, or sold their soul to the adrenochrome club to further their careers. We don't enjoy the same music anymore, because we know that in order to become more than a one hit wonder, most have sold out. Also, as mentioned previously, the frequency of the music has been set to deliberately lower our vibration. We don't enjoy the same foods any longer, because as our frequency rises, and our bodies become more crystalline, food doesn't taste the same. We don't trust food anymore, as we are now much more aware of the poison and chemicals deliberately put into our foods, and we are also learning that many processed foods are at the best cacogenic and at the worse hold the potential to contain human remains! We can't just enjoy a straight forward day out site seeing in cities, museums or art galleries, because we know history is a lie, we know much of our Tartarian architecture has been decimated, and we know that the art industry has been a "legitimate" cover for money laundering for the child-trafficking/adrenochrome industry. So much to take in, on so many levels. For me, literally nothing looks, feels, sounds or tastes the same anymore, and I was relatively aware of most of this stuff before, so I can't imagine how bewildering it may seem to those that have relatively recently woken up.

Undoubtedly, one way or another we will all go through a grieving process, as we move from the old 3D paradigm to the new 5D earth. My years of experience as a psychotherapist has helped me to understand that everyone will have a unique experience of grief, and my therapeutic advice would be to just be gentle with yourselves, allow whatever comes up for you to come up, don't try to change it, or try to fit it to a model that you think is acceptable. The key is to allow the emotions, thoughts, and any physical sensations to play out. Notice them, acknowledge they are there, feel them, but don't make any judgement of yourself because of them, then move on. Don't get stuck in the emotion. The trick is, simply allow the emotion to pass through you, then put your focus of attention onto something that brings you joy. Much of our human experience is based on the fact we are able to feel emotions. However, it is not wise to hold onto these emotions, in 3D, many common diseases have an emotional component, most commonly holding on to a disruptive emotions, such as fear, guilt, anger. It's time that we let go of all this emotional baggage and step into a space of trusting God.

Trust in God – Many of us are experiencing the losses as mentioned above, and even though we are working hard at manifesting aspects of our 5D lives, in reality many of us currently are living in the chaos of the 4th dimension. The bridge between the two worlds, neither here or there, and that is exactly how it feels sometimes! On the one hand the illusion and fake safety we felt in our former 3D existence has been shattered, now that we can see through the lies and the fog of the spiritual war we have been fighting. And yet, we are not yet fully stepped into our 5D lives. We may be filp flopping between the two, sometimes seeing clearly our 5D potentials, then other times feeling very 3D and viewing our 5D future as merely "hopium", or a fanciful illusion. Or we may feel plagued with uncertainty, in "no mans land" territory.

It is at this point, that our faith in our higher selves, and God are really put to the test. I liken it to bungee jumping. It feels like I am about to jump of a cliff, into the vast unknown, there is no way back to 3D, I feel compelled to make the paradigm shift. Yet despite my prophetic visions, my inner knowledge, and my spiritual journeying, to be absolutely truthful, it is still a great unknown for all of us. I know it is going to be wonderful, and we are going to be reclaiming the lives that are rightfully ours, but to change paradigm whilst still incarnated in bodies is a brand new concept for planet earth, switching from 3D to 5D has never been done before. The thing I need to have most faith in when jumping off the cliff is the rope that is going to hold me. The rope being God. It all comes down to letting go, and having complete trust in God. It's been a long hard journey, but I am now ready.............see you on the other side!

The Goddess and the God

The Goddess and the God
Got together one day
A tryst in the midst
A Tussle in the hay

They came together as one
Two creator beings
Magical alchemy
A planet was begun

Throughout the ages
They incarnated on earth
To oversee the consciousness
Of the planet they had birthed

It was all going
So perfectly well
Until the lizards landed
And created living hell

The Goddess and the God
Had to up their game
By daily battling demons
Any denying lizards their reign

It was a long hard battle
But in the end God won
And now they're taking respite
In the centre of the sun

Gillian England

MYSTIC HEALING THERAPIES

My name is Gillian I live in England,
I am a natural mystic, healer, author, psychotherapist,
spiritual teacher and energy director.

My mission is to assist in the developing consciousness of the human race,
as well as to bring in divine energy codes to the planet..

A graduate of the University of Derby, I have worked as a psychotherapist for over 20 years. Prior
to that I was a Butlin's red coat, professional dancer and fire-eater. My heartfelt desire is to help
people help themselves, by assisting them to step into their divine power. Sometimes people
need a little assistance, be it releasing them from prior contracts, spells, entity attachments, or
connecting them to their star heritage or higher selves. Mystic Healing Therapies can be the
gateway to this, I will see you, and honour your experience, whatever that might be.

www.gillianengland.com

You can also find me on youtube and telegram

Gillian England

MYSTIC HEALING THERAPIES

Also available as part of the 'Road to Enchantment Series' is
BOOK ONE 'Enchanted Earth'

www.gillianengland.com

Made in the USA
Columbia, SC
20 October 2023

24305071R00048